Bologna
Massa-Carrara
Garfagnana
Lucca
Pistoia
Prato
Chocolate Valley
Mugello
Florence
Pisa
Arezzo
Chianti
Livorno
Siena
Val di Chiana
Montepulciano
Montalcino
Elba
Maremma
Grosseto

The Silver Spoon

tuscany

A TUSCAN JOURNEY

Previous page:
Cypress trees, rolling hills with vineyards, and olive groves make up the peaceful Tuscan landscape.

Everyone has their own idea of Tuscany, even those who have never visited the region. Renowned the world over for its culture and history, Tuscany is as much about the ancient olive groves, rustic farmhouses and lines of cypress trees in the early morning mist as it is about the beautiful paintings, exquisite sculptures, medieval towns and architectural masterpieces.

But the reality of Tuscany is more complex than this rose-tinted idea. There are few places in the world where the locals would see no contradiction in referring to themselves as *mangiafagioli* (bean-eaters) while in the same breath, and without a trace of conceit, telling you that they gave the world such men of genius as Michelangelo and Leonardo da Vinci.

Nowhere is the essence of Tuscany better expressed than in its cuisine. Always an aspect of life in the region, today Tuscany's cuisine elicits almost as much interest and praise as its artistic and cultural heritage. Its reputation for quality, simplicity and flavour is recognized around the world. But just what is Tuscan cuisine?

It is the legacy of two distinct traditions — those of the countryside and the city. Peasant cooking was born out of poverty and necessity, and is characterized by the resourcefulness of a culture that adapted and learned to make the most of what the land had to offer. From the city comes the cuisine of the nobility, with all the trappings of wealth and grandeur that one would expect from cities as splendid as Florence, Siena and Pisa. This dual identity is still evident today, and Tuscany's noble past is reflected in the universally recognized Florentine-style steak (see page 138), known to the locals as simply a steak or a *fiorentina*. And yet the magic of Tuscany is that true Florentines would be equally satisfied with a simple *panino* (sandwich) stuffed with

The historic *borghi* (towns) of Siena, with their unspoilt and often traffic-free streets, have remained almost unchanged in six hundred years.

TRATTORIA
MAZZONI
Alimentari Trattoria

A typical family-run trattoria in Arezzo, Mazzoni continues to serve simple, rustic local dishes.

tripe and eaten on the go, perhaps under the watchful gaze of Michelangelo's *David*.

Over the centuries, the one constant feature of Tuscan cuisine is that it has remained faithful to its roots. Territory and the Tuscan table are, and always have been, synonymous. From the towering Apennine and Apuan mountain ranges, across a landscape of rolling hills, forests, olive groves and vines, to the coast and the waters of the Tyrrhenian Sea, the flavours of territory speak out in every dish. The traditions and culture of the countryside remain intact, a living heritage of times gone by. Olives are still hand-harvested as they were a thousand years ago, and pecorino cheese is still produced using the same techniques as those used by the Romans. Chianina cattle still roam freely in the Val di Chiana, the shepherds from Zeri still watch over their flocks as they graze in the high Apennine pastures, and farmers in Arezzo still cultivate zolfino beans in the same time-honoured fashion as their predecessors did centuries ago.

Oblivious to modern fads and trends, the essentials of the Tuscan table remain the same. Hearty soups prevail, taking full advantage of locally grown pulses (legumes), grains, fresh vegetables and foraged ingredients. Leaving nothing to waste, tougher cuts of meat are still cooked slowly, transformed with love, care and patience into meltingly tender stews, while the finer cuts and joints are reserved for special occasions, roasted with wild aromatic herbs or briefly seared over hot coals and finished with a drizzle of olive oil. Along the coastline fish remains important and the tasty fish stew *Cacciucco alla Livornese* (Livornese-style cacciucco, see page 182) is a popular reminder of a humble past.

Following page:
Olive trees, with their silvery leaves and gnarled trunks, can bear fruit for more than a thousand years.

The starting point for any Tuscan meal is, as it always has been, the gastronomic 'holy trinity': wine, olive oil and bread. The wine speaks for itself. With Chianti Classico, Brunello di Montalcino and the 'Super Tuscans' (a class of superior wines such as Tignanello and Sassicaia labeled *Vino da Tavola*, or table wine) representing some of the oldest wine traditions in Europe, it should hardly come as a surprise that Tuscan wines are regarded as among the world's best. Whether as an ingredient to flavour the local *salami*, a base to a stew, or a treat in which to dip and flavour a *Cantucci* (see page 115), wine is to the locals something much more than just an accompaniment to a fine meal.

Then there is the olive oil, whose colour and perfume evoke memories of the unspoiled landscape and ancient olive groves from which it was made. From the strong, piquant oils of Chianti and Siena to the delicate oils of Lucca, each region's product has its own character. This versatility is reflected in its use in the Tuscan kitchen. Whether an essential ingredient in a simple dish of *Fagioli nel fiasco* (Beans in a flask, see page 267), a finishing touch to a humble *Ribollita* (see page 234) or an extravagant *Bistecca alla fiorentina* (Florentine-style steak, see page 138), the legendary 'c' shape of oil drizzled over a Tuscan dish has almost become a standard unit of measurement.

Finally there is the bread, the cornerstone of Tuscan cooking. It is always made without salt because, as the Tuscans know all too well, it will be eaten alongside very flavourful food, so less is more. It would be unthinkable to serve a Tuscan meal without bread, just as it would be inconceivable for a Tuscan cook to throw out bread that others might consider past its best. *Pane raffermo* — literally 'stale bread' — has innumerable uses, from *crostini* to the addition to soups and stews to soak up the juices. When it is eaten fresh it forms the perfect accompaniment to the fine cured meats and cheeses made throughout the region.

Bread and the finest olive oil are the cornerstones of Tuscan cuisine.

Although other traditional styles of cooking have withered, Tuscan cuisine has endured and flourished. Like the countryside and traditions from which it was born, it has survived the test of time relatively intact. Whether using up leftovers, turning under-appreciated cuts of meat into something delectable or transforming the humblest bean into a delicious soup, such resourcefulness is characteristic of people who take nothing for granted. This is the essence of Tuscan cuisine and the essence of Tuscany.

FOOD FESTIVALS

Tuscans take great pride in their gastronomic heritage and that pride is expressed throughout the year at the *sagra*, or festival. The term is often used interchangeably with *festa* or *feste* (festival or festivals), but generally, in Italy, if you talk to someone about going to a *sagra*, it is understood that you are going to an event to eat.

These informal festivals are open to everyone and have a strong familial and community feel. There are no reservations, no private tables and the plates, cutlery and glasses will usually be plastic. However, for a small fee (less than what you would pay for the same dish in a restaurant) what you get in return is a true slice of Tuscan life: a great setting, an excellent home-cooked meal and, of course, a chance to sample a few glasses of what the locals produce in the way of wine.

Finding a *sagra* is seldom difficult, especially in the summer months. With such a rich and varied gastronomic tradition, there is generally a *sagra* on somewhere, wherever you happen to be staying. Some are seasonal events linked to the annual agrarian calendar, such as the Luccese festivals, *Fiera del vino novello* (New wine fair) held every November or the *Fiera dei fiori e dei dolci di Santa Zita* (Flower and dessert fair of Santa Zita) in April. From harvesting grapes, or bottling a new wine to the opening of the fishing or

Fresh produce on display outside a local *alimentari* (grocer's shop).

Most meals are concluded simply with a piece of fresh fruit, grown and picked locally.

hunting season, there's no shortage of good excuses to hold a festival.

Others celebrate a particular dish of the area such as the *Sagra della fett'unta* (Fett'unta [a lightly oiled slice of bread] festival) in Montecatini Terme, Pistoia; the *Sagra della ribollita* (Ribollita festival) in Loro Ciuffienna, Arezzo; and the *Sagra del neccio* (Neccio [chestnut flat bread] festival) held in Pescia, Pistoia. Most of the region's famed dishes are represented somewhere with a *sagra*, and when a dish's provenance is disputed, two or more towns will sometimes even host separate events.

Finally, there are the festivals held to celebrate a regional product or speciality such as the famed *Sagra del tartufo* (Truffle festival) held in San Miniato every October or the *Sagra del lardo di Colonnata* (Lardo di Colonnata festival) held in the town of the same name, usually in August.

Pages 20—21:
A timeless and unmistakable portrait of the Tuscan countryside: undulating rolling hills dotted with the occasional stone farmhouse and accompanying row of cypress trees.

FOOD FESTIVALS

JANUARY

Cioccolosità | Chocolate festival
Monsummano Terme, Pistoia

Fiera del cioccolato | Chocolate fair
Florence, Florence

FEBRUARY

Pulendina | Polenta festival
Vernio, Prato

MARCH

Sagra del neccio | Chestnut flat bread festival
Pescia, Pistoia

Capodanno fiorentino | Florentine sweets and cakes festival
Florence, Florence

Festa dei fichi | Figs festival
Vicchio, Florence

Choccolandia | Chocolate festival
Cecina, Livorno

APRIL

Fiera dei fiori e dei dolci de Santa Zita | Flower and dessert fair of Santa Zita
Lucca, Lucca

Enolia | Olive oil festival
Seravezza, Lucca

Festa della farina dolce | Cake flour festival
Piteglio, Pistoia

Sagra del cinghiale | Wild boar festival
Certaldo, Florence

Sagra del carciofo | Purple artichoke festival
Piombino, Livorno

Sagra dell'agnello | Lamb festival
Manciano, Grosseto

MAY

Sagra della porchetta | Roast pork festival
Valenza, Massa Carrara

Sagra del polliglio | Chicken and rabbit festival
Montespertoli, Florence

Festa del pane | Bread festival
Certaldo, Florence

Mostra del Chianti | Chianti wine fair
Montespertoli, Florence

Sagra del prosciutto e baccelli | Prosciutto and broad beans festival
Boschi di Lari, Pisa

Sagra del pecorino | Pecorino cheese festival
Saturnia, Grosseto

Sagra dei pici | Pici festival
Celle sul Rigo, Siena

Sapori delle Crete Senesi | Flavours of the crete senesi
Chiusure, Arbia and Asciano, Siena

Settimana dei vino | Wine tasting
Siena, Siena

JUNE

Festa del grano | Grain festival
Fivizzano, Massa-Carrara

Festa della pecora zerasca | Zerasca sheep festival
Zeri, Massa Carrara

Sagra dell'oliva dolce | Sweet olive festival
Capannori, Lucca

Sagra del cacciucco | Cacciucco festival
Rufina, Florence

Sagra della bruschetta | Bruschetta festival
Campi Bisenzio, Florence

Sagra del pinola | Pine nut festival
San Casciano Val di Pesa, Florence

Sagra delle ciliegie | Cherry festival
Lari, Pisa

Sagra della pastasciutta | Pasta festival
Cortona, Arezzo

JULY

Sagra del pinolo | Pine nut festival
San Piero a Grado, Pisa

Sagra del fungo porcino | Porcini mushroom festival
Scarperia, Florence

Sagra del pesce | Fish festival
Piombino, Livorno

Sagra del cinghiale | Wild boar festival
Rispescia, Grosseto

Sagra del cacciucco | Cacciucco festival
Renzino, Arezzo

Sagra della ribollita | Ribollita festival
Loro Ciuffenna, Arezzo

AUGUST

Sagra del lardo di Colonnata | Lardo di Colonnata festival
Colonnata, Massa Carrara

Festa del fagiolo di Sorana | Sorana bean festival
Sorana, Pescia, Pistoia

Sagra del buongustaio | Pleasures of food and wine festival
San Gimignano, Siena

Sagra della polenta | Polenta festival
Manciano, Grosseto

Sagra della trippa | Tripe festival
Vallerona, Grosseto

Sagra della bistecca | Chianina beef festival
Cortona, Arezzo

Sagra del fungo porcino | Porcini mushroom festival
Corezzo, Arezzo

SEPTEMBER

Sagra del fico | Dried figs festival
Bacchereto, Prato

Sagra della polenta, dei porcini e del cinghiale | Polenta, mushrooms and wild boar festival
Poggio alla Malva, Prato

Rassegna del Chianti Classico | Chianti Classico wine festival
Greve in Chianti, Florence

Sagra dell'anatra muta | Wild duck festival
Empoli, Florence

Settimana del miele | Honey week
Montalcino, Siena

Sagra del vin santo e del ciambello | Vin Santo and cake festival
Valiano di Montepulciano, Siena

Sagra del porcino | Porcino festival
Pievescola, Siena

Fiera del cacio | Pecorino festival
Pienza, Siena

Sagra della porchetta | Porchetta festival
Monte San Savino, Arezzo

OCTOBER

Festa della castagna | Chestnut festival
Seravezza, Lucca

Festa del vino nuovo | First wine of the vintage festival
Artimino, Prato

NOVEMBER

Fiera del vino novello | New wine festival
Montecarlo, Lucca

Festa dell'olio | Olive festival
Montemurlo, Prato

Sagra del tartufo | Truffle festival
Scarperia, Florence

Mostra mercato nazionale del tartufo bianco di San Miniato | National exhibition of the white truffle of San Miniato
San Miniato, Pisa

DECEMBER

Sagra di Suvereto | Feast of Suvereto
Suvereto, Grosseto

I

MASSA-CARRARA

Nestled between Liguria to the north, Emilia-Romagna to the east and the Tyrrhenian Sea to the west, Massa-Carrara is Tuscany's northernmost province, and is predominantly mountainous. Much of it falls within an area known as the Lunigiana, which literally means the 'land of the moon'. It takes its name from the ancient town of Luni, a Roman settlement established in 177 BC that was once the principal town on the northern Tuscan coast. Some claim that the name Luni refers to the fact that the moon's beauty is enhanced when framed against the stunning backdrop of the white-peaked Apuan Alps and the towering Apennine mountains.

Previous page:
The marble in the Apuan Alps has been excavated since Roman times.

Of all the Tuscan provinces, Massa-Carrara remains the least discovered. It is perhaps best known for its exquisite white marble, which has been excavated from the Apuan Alps overlooking Carrara for over two thousand years. From the Marble Arch in London to Trajan's Column in Rome, Carrara marble has been used to fashion some of the world's most distinguished and best-known sculpture and architecture. The marble industry has always been fundamental to the local economy. It also lends a hand in the production of one of the province's most celebrated dishes, *lardo di Colonnata* (see page 32), a product made from pork fat, which is spiced and then cured in marble basins.

Resourcefulness in using whatever is to hand has always been a defining feature of the province's cuisine. The cuisines of the cities of Massa and Carrara, where some sixty per cent of the province's population live, have much in common. Since they are both near the coast, the flavours of both mountains and sea — *monti e mare* — are discernible. Oily fish, such as sardines, anchovies and mackerel, are used in abundance. The preparation is always simple — a popular local dish consists of fresh anchovies, cleaned, dusted lightly in flour, dipped in egg and pan-fried. Up in the mountains, the difficult terrain has always meant that every opportunity had to be exploited to the full.

The cheeses made in and around Fivizzano (using milk from sheep and goats that graze in the high mountain pastures) are examples of the mountain people's ability to maximize whatever the land has to offer, which in turn has shaped the area's cuisine. An unconventional mix of chestnut and wheat flours is even used to make the pasta dough. It is said that the proportions of the mix are determined by the skill of the housewife and the shelf life of the flour available.

Finally, the cakes in the area are delicious and well worth seeking out. There is always a good selection, made fresh daily, at the Antica Pasticceria degli Svizzeri in the historic centre of Lunigiana's capital, Pontremoli, a small mountain town on the border with Emilia-Romagna. The family has been baking here since 1842 and still follow traditional recipes using a recipe book from 1841. The original Art Nouveau-style *caffè* is a favourite haunt of the locals, who exchange the latest gossip over an espresso and perhaps a *pasteriala* (an almond cake), or a tasty *amor di Pontremoli*, a marshmallowy cream sandwiched between two wafers.

TESTAROLI

Of ancient, probably Roman, origins, the *testo* is a flat cast-iron or terracotta griddle with a large domed lid. Traditionally a *testo* could be found in every household in Lunigiana, and such was the importance of these cooking pots that in 1391 the city of Pontremoli levied a tax on them. The *testo* had multiple uses, such as for roasting meats or baking savoury vegetable tarts, but it is most commonly associated with the preparation of *Testaroli* (see page 28), a type of large pancake (crêpe), which is approximately 40–45 centimetres (16–18 inches) in diameter and a few millimetres thick. They are made from a mixture of flour (originally farro flour, see page 64), water and salt, which is then cut into small diamonds, boiled and served hot, most often with a pesto sauce. In the autumn, when local porcini mushrooms are in season, they are served with a mushroom sauce. A number of food historians have claimed that *testaroli* were a forerunner of pasta.

In the village of Podenzana, a smaller version of *testaroli,* known locally as *panigacci,* are made. These are not boiled but reheated over a fire until crisp, and served hot with soft cheeses and cold meats such as Parma ham and salami. They can also be smothered with a hazelnut and chocolate spread.

Left:
Alberto Bellotti is one of only three artisans who continue to make *testaroli* in the traditional way.

Opposite:
The 25 kg (55 lb) cast-iron *testo* is heated over flames and used to cook the batter.

TESTAROLI AL PESTO

Testaroli with pesto sauce

This dish was traditionally cooked over hot coals in a large, shallow dish with a domed lid made either of terracotta or cast-iron called a *testo*.

Preparation time: 40 minutes
Cooking time: 20 minutes
Serves 6

For the pesto sauce:
— 50 (1 cup) basil leaves
— 1 clove garlic
— 40 g (⅓ cup) pine nuts
— 2 tablespoons walnuts
— 80 – 150 ml (⅓ – ⅔ cup) extra-virgin olive oil
— 40 g (½ cup) grated pecorino cheese
— 40 g (½ cup) grated Parmesan cheese
— salt

For the testaroli:
— 375 g (3 ¼ cups) plain (all-purpose) flour
— salt

First, make the pesto sauce. Put the basil, garlic, pine nuts and walnuts in a mortar and pound with a pestle until smooth and thoroughly combined. Gradually stir in the oil, grated cheeses and a pinch of salt, if necessary.

Sift the flour with a pinch of salt into a bowl and gradually stir in 720 ml (3 cups) water to make a smooth batter. Pour the batter into a traditional Italian *testo* (see page 26) or non-stick frying pan or skillet with a lid. Cover and cook over hot coals or on medium-high heat for about 2 minutes on each side.

Remove the pancake from the dish and cut into diamond shapes about 3 cm (1¼ inches) long on each side. Continue until all the batter is used up.

Bring a large pan of salted water to a boil. Add the testaroli, bring back to a boil and cook for only 2 minutes. Drain and serve immediately with the pesto sauce.

POLENTA PASTICCIATA CON IL SUGO FINTO

Layered polenta with vegetable sauce

Polenta, as we know it today, appeared during the eighteenth century and quickly became an important staple in the diets of poor farmers. Highly versatile and popular, it can be eaten as a *piatto unico* (one plate dish), soft as an accompaniment to stews or sliced and fried once cooled.

Preparation time: 40 minutes
Cooking time: 1 hour
Serves 4

For the sauce:

- 500 g (1 lb 2 oz) ripe tomatoes, peeled, seeded and chopped
- 4 tablespoons olive oil
- 2 celery stalks, finely chopped
- 1 carrot, finely chopped
- 1 onion, finely chopped
- 1 sprig flat-leaf parsley, finely chopped
- 1 sprig basil, finely chopped
- 100 g (generous 1 cup) grated Parmesan cheese
- salt and pepper

For the polenta:

- 2 teaspoons salt
- 400 g (2 ¾ cups) polenta

To make the sauce, press the tomatoes through a sieve (sifter) into a bowl. Heat the oil in a pan. Add the celery, carrot, onion, parsley and basil and cook over low heat, stirring occasionally, for 5 minutes, until softened. Stir in the tomatoes, season with salt and pepper, half cover the pan and simmer for 1 hour.

Meanwhile, make the polenta. Pour 2.25 litres (10 cups) lukewarm water into a heavy pan, add the salt and bring to a boil. While stirring constantly, sprinkle in the polenta and cook, stirring frequently and vigorously, for 30–40 minutes, until thickened and smooth.

Make alternate layers of polenta, the vegetable mixture and grated Parmesan in a preheated serving dish and serve hot.

LARDO DI COLONNATA

This cured and spiced pork fat is one of the true treasures of Tuscan cuisine. It has been made in Colonnata, a tiny mining village set in the foothills of the Apuan Alps, since Roman times. The village sits alongside the quarries of Carrara, the source of the marble that Michelangelo used to carve his *David* and other masterpieces. The same material is indispensable to the production of *lardo*. The pork back fat is layered in white marble troughs — *conche* as they are called locally — on a bed of salt and a mixture of herbs and spices, which includes rosemary, oregano, sage, garlic, pepper, nutmeg, cinnamon and cloves. Every family uses its own special mix, a closely guarded secret that is passed down from one generation to the next.

Many attempts have been made to imitate *lardo di Colonnata*, but they have always fallen short. The curing technique is completely natural, with no artificial additives or preservatives, and its distinctive character is derived entirely from local environmental conditions. The microclimate of the underground caves, along with the porous nature of the marble, make this a product that cannot easily be replicated.

Today, *lardo di Colonnata* is considered a delicacy and some purists argue that it is best enjoyed thinly sliced and served simply on a wooden platter as an antipasto in its own right. Traditionally, however, it was eaten as a *companatico* (an accompaniment to bread) — this was the marble quarrymen's daily fodder, and being high in calories it helped to ward off the cold. Also, as a product born from necessity, its uses were many and varied. Today, the people of Colonnata still melt it to use as a substitute for butter or oil in cooking, for example to sauté vegetables or to add depth and flavour to a stew. *Lardo di Colonnata* can also be sliced and wrapped around fish before skewering it and cooking it over hot embers, or around a joint of meat before roasting it.

With its unique colour and textural variations, marble has always been a highly prized and valued stone. The marble of Carrara has been essential to the area's economy for centuries.

Following pages:
(Page 34) Lardo di colonnata producer, Venanzio Vannucci. The lard is aged naturally in warm underground caves and cured for a minimum of six months.

(Page 35) The lard is prepared only during the cooler months of the year, from September to May. Once cured, the delicacy can be served as an antipasto.

ZERI LAMB

Zerasca sheep, a hardy breed native to Lunigiana, are raised high in the rugged mountains above the remote village of Zeri in northwestern Massa-Carrara. The semi-wild flocks graze for the better part of the year on unpolluted mountain pastures more than 800 metres (2,600 feet) above sea level. In the coldest months of winter, they are brought down to the sheepfold and fed on hay from the same pastures. Since there are only some three thousand of these animals, the breed is considered rare, and therefore breeding is strictly regulated. All the farms in the area are small family ventures, with flocks ranging from 50 to 250 sheep.

The Zerasca sheep take shelter in the fold during the coldest months of winter.

The ewes' milk, which feeds their lambs, is very high in protein, and this, in addition to the herbs and grasses from the mountain pastures, no doubt contributes to the distinctive texture and flavour of Zeri lamb, which is very tender, slightly sweet and fragrant. Although it is highly prized, the meat is relatively scarce, and therefore much of it is only distributed locally to restaurants or shops. The lamb is delicious fried, in stews, cooked *alla brace* (on the grill) or, most traditionally, roasted in a *testo* in the oven with potatoes. It is usually accompanied by local red wine.

Following page:
Sheep grazing and breeding have become widespread throughout Tuscany since the time of the Etruscans.

AGNELLO AL TESTO

Lamb in a 'testo'

Preparation time: 30 minutes
Cooking time: 1 hour + 15 minutes for resting
Serves 6

- 30 g (2 oz) lardo, preferably from Colonnata
- 3 sage leaves
- 2 cloves garlic
- 1 sprig rosemary
- 1 × 1.5-kg (3 ¼-lb) leg of lamb
- 1 kg (2 ¼ lb) potatoes, peeled and diced into 2.5 cm (1 inch) cubes
- 50 ml (scant ¼ cup) olive oil
- 50 ml (scant ¼ cup) dry white wine
- 1 bay leaf
- salt and pepper

This dish was traditionally cooked over hot coals in a large, shallow dish with a domed lid made either of terracotta or cast-iron called a *testo*. You could use a chimenea or kettle barbecue. Otherwise, preheat the oven to 200°C/400°F/Gas Mark 6. Chop together the lardo, sage, garlic and rosemary. Using a small sharp knife, make small incisions into the skin of the lamb and insert the herb mix into them. Season the meat generously with salt and pepper.

Spread out the potatoes in a *testo* or a casserole. Add the olive oil, wine and bay leaf and put the lamb on top. Cover and after an hour, remove the casserole from the oven and allow the lamb to rest for 15 minutes. Remove the potatoes from the casserole, drain on kitchen paper (paper towel), season with salt and cook on a baking sheet for a further 15 minutes.

Roasting time for the lamb should be 1 hour for rare, 1¼ hours for medium, 1½ hours for well done.

CONIGLIO ALLE MELE

Rabbit with apples

Preparation time: 30 minutes + 2 hours for marinating
Cooking time: 45 minutes
Serves 4–6

- 100 g (3 ½ oz) slices of rigatino or pancetta, cut into thin strips
- 1 × 2.25–2.75-kg (5–6-lb) skinned and cleaned rabbit, liver reserved
- 1 kg (2 ¼ lb) Pippin or other sharp apples
- 1 litre (4 ½ cups) dry white wine
- 150 ml (⅔ cup) Vin Santo wine
- 1 tablespoon fennel seeds
- 50 g (4 tablespoons) butter
- 2 tablespoons olive oil
- 2 large onions, very finely chopped
- salt and pepper

Using a larding needle, thread strips of rigatino or pancetta through the rabbit. Season the cavity with salt and pepper. Peel, core and chop enough apples to fill the cavity (the quantity will depend on the size of the rabbit) and then sew up the opening with trussing thread or kitchen string. Pour the white wine and half the Vin Santo into a shallow dish, add the fennel seeds and put the rabbit on top. Cover and let marinate for at least 2 hours.

Melt half the butter with the oil in a large, shallow pan. Add the onions and cook over low heat, stirring occasionally, for 5 minutes, until softened. Meanwhile, remove the rabbit from the marinade and pat dry with paper towels. Add the rabbit to the pan, increase the heat to medium and cook, turning frequently, for 5–8 minutes, until evenly browned. Pour in half the marinade and cook until the alcohol has evaporated.

Reduce the heat, cover and simmer for 15 minutes. Meanwhile, peel, core and slice the remaining apples.

Add them to the pan and, if necessary, add the remaining marinade. Re-cover the pan and simmer for another 15 minutes, or until the meat is cooked and tender.

Trim and chop the liver. Melt the remaining butter in a small frying pan. Add the liver and cook over medium heat, stirring frequently, for a few minutes, until lightly browned. Drizzle with the remaining Vin Santo and cook until the alcohol has evaporated. Season with salt and pepper and cook for a few minutes more. Lift the rabbit out of the pan and cut into pieces. Place on a warmed serving dish and garnish with the sliced apples and liver mixture. Serve immediately.

HONEY FROM LUNIGIANA

Perhaps the best example of the harmonious relationship between land and food production in the Lunigiana region is the production of its famous local honey. Beekeeping has been a tradition here for centuries, and it remains so in a landscape largely untouched by development and industrialization. The earliest documented evidence of honey production in the area is a tax assessment form dated 1508, which lists it as an income-producing activity, and thus subject to taxation. Hundreds of years later, *miele della Lunigiana* was the first honey in Italy to achieve European PDO (Protected Designation of Origin) status, which was awarded to the two types of honey produced in the fourteen communes of Lunigiana: chestnut and acacia.

Today, honey still features heavily in Tuscan cuisine. Lunigiana honey is delicious simply eaten on its own, but it is also excellent drizzled over a piece of fresh pecorino cheese or used in the preparation of regional specialities such as *Panforte* (see page 244), a flat spiced cake made with honey, nuts and dried fruits. It is also used in making *Spongata* (see page 46), a rich, honeyed nut and raisin cake that is wrapped between two layers of pastry and traditionally eaten over the Christmas holidays. Although this cake is often typically asso-ciated with the provinces of Parma, Piacenza and Reggio Emilia in Emilia-Romagna, the *spongata* of Pontremoli (which is one of the few places where it is still made by hand using traditional techniques) is held in high regard.

Wild mountain flowers and blossoms flourish in the unpolluted mountains of the Lunigiana, providing the perfect natural habitat for bees and butterflies.

SPONGATA DI PONTREMOLI

Spongata from Pontremoli

Preparation time: 1 hour + 24 hours for standing
Cooking time: 30 minutes
Serves 4

For the filling:

- 230 g (scant 1 cup) clear honey
- 50 ml (¼ cup) white wine
- 50 g (½ cup) pine nuts
- 60 g (½ cup) sultanas
- 100 g (scant 1 cup) dry biscuits, crushed
- 1 teaspoon bitter cocoa powder

For the pastry:

- 300 g (2 ¾ cup) flour
- 100 g (scant 1 cup) sugar
- 150 g (⅔ cup) unsalted butter, softened
- 3 tablespoons white wine
- 1 small beaten egg

Make the filling by gently heating the honey with the wine. When runny, add the pine nuts, sultanas, crushed biscuits and cocoa powder. Mix everything together well, transfer to a bowl and leave in a cool place for 24 hours or overnight.

The following day, preheat the oven to 180°C / 360°F/ Gas Mark 4. Make the pastry by combining together the flour, sugar, softened butter and wine. Knead together well until a smooth dough is formed, then divide into two equal pieces. Roll out the first piece into a circle approximately ½ cm (¼ inch) thick and place it on a piece of kitchen parchment directly on a baking sheet. Add the filling to the middle of the pastry and spread evenly leaving a border of about 2 cm (¾ inch). Roll out the remaining piece of pastry into a circle of the same dimension and place this on top. Seal together the edges by crimping them with your finger and thumb. Brush with a beaten egg and make a few holes on top with the end of a wooden spoon. Bake for 30–35 minutes. Allow to cool and serve.

II

LUCCA

Every year over one million spectators descend on the seaside town of Viareggio in Lucca to watch a colourful, noisy parade of papier-mâché floats circle the 2-kilometre (1½-mile) seafront route known locally as *La Passeggiata* — a renowned carnival held since 1873.

Previous page:
The province of Lucca is renowned for its charming villages, hilly landscapes and a temperate climate — making it an ideal destination around the year.

The excesses of carnival contrast starkly with the cuisine of the mountainous Garfagnana region, situated on the eastern side of Lucca province. Here the cuisine is simple and substantial, the rhythms of the old life having left little time for the preparation of elaborate dishes. Life in the area was hard, the inhospitable terrain and infertile soils forcing inhabitants to adapt to their environment. What natural resources the land had to offer were, and still are, utilized to the full, as seen for example in the locally produced chestnut flours, honeys and cheeses. It is also seen in the hearty, robust soups, which are typical of the region. Soups such as *Minestra garfagnina di farro* (Garfagnina farro soup, see page 66) were reflections of what the territory naturally had to offer.

Moving westwards to the forests of the Versilia and the coast, the rustic mountainous fare gives way to flavours of the sea and the land.

Along Lucca's coastline, fish plays an important role, both in the local economy and in the gastronomy. In Viareggio the fish market is a constant source of bustling activity and good seafood restaurants abound. Local specialities include the excellent *viareggio cacciucco* (a less spicy take on the *cacciucco*, the famous fish stew from Livorno, see page 182) and the famed *trabaccolara con spaghetti* (spaghetti with king prawns). This dish owes its name to the vessel used by the fishermen from the coastal town of San Benedetto del Tronto in Abruzzo (a region in central Italy), some of whom moved to the area in the 20s and late 30s. It was born as a poor man's dish as it was traditionally made with the fish that remained unsold at the market.

Back in the city of Lucca, it is customary to end a meal with a slice of *buccellato* (a sweet ring-shaped cake with raisins and aniseed) and a glass of Vin Santo to dip it in. The original recipe of the city's most famed cake is held by the Taddeucci family which has been producing the *buccellato* from their bakery in Piazza S. Michele since 1881. There's an old folk saying which goes: '*Chi va a Lucca e non mangia il buccellato è come se non ci fosse stato*', which loosely translates into 'Anyone who comes to Lucca and doesn't eat *buccellato* hasn't come here at all'.

Following page:
A panoramic view of Lucca from above. The *coppe* (terracotta roof tiles) were traditionally made by hand.

OLIVE OIL

The olive has been cultivated in Lucca since the time of the Etruscans. The olives are harvested between November and January and the first pressing is considered to produce the finest oil.

Both as an ingredient and as a finishing touch it would be difficult, if not impossible, to imagine the Tuscan kitchen without Tuscan olive oil. In Lucca, the landscape resembles a patchwork quilt of olive groves and vineyards. Clues to the importance of olives to the area's economy, history and cultural heritage are everywhere, even in the road signs. 'Oliveto', 'Olivetecci' and 'Ulettori' point towards towns whose very names are reference to the olive tree.

Lucca's olive oil has always been high quality. In fact, such was its reputation and fame that as early as the 1800s it was sought after in the USA, making it one of the first culinary products to be exported to America from Tuscany. A wealth of documentation, dating as far back as the eleventh century, sets out an impressive body of rules and regulations controlling the production and sale of Lucchese olive oil. In one such document, dated 12 January 1241, farmers were limited to the sale of 10 kg (22 lb) of oil in any given year. If the quality was poor, the limit was reduced to 7 kg (15 lb), the difference being compensated for the following year. The legacy of this strict history of regulation can still be felt in the quality of today's product.

What makes Lucca's olive oil different from others is its delicate flavour. Generally less aggressive than other Tuscan oils, these from Lucca owe their distinctive character to the high concentration of Frantoio, an olive variety with a particularly delicate and perfumed taste. Lucca's oil is slightly fruity on the palate, light to medium flavour and remarkably balanced, making it highly versatile.

Following pages:
Olives are still harvested using traditional methods. Cloths are wrapped around the trunks to catch and gather the olives as they are picked from the trees.

CAVOLO NERO

Also known as black leaf kale or black cabbage, cavolo nero is much used in Tuscan cuisine and is an essential ingredient in many of the region's favourite dishes. There are two main types of cavolo nero grown in Tuscany: *cavolo nero di Lucca* and *cavolo riccio nero di Toscana*. The latter is grown mainly in the provinces of Florence and Arezzo. The cavolo nero of Lucca has been grown in the region since the 1800s. It is harvested by hand, and methods of cultivation have not changed over the years. In both size and appearance it differs from the *cavolo riccio* grown elsewhere in Tuscany.

Unlike many kinds of cabbage, cavolo nero does not form a central head. Its leaves, which resemble palm fronds, are a deep greenish black, can grow up to a metre (3 feet) long, and have pronounced ribs and surfaces with a distinctive bubbly appearance. Cavolo nero is a highly nutritious vegetable, rich in vitamins A, B, C, D and E, copper, manganese and calcium. It is also bursting with antioxidants, low in calories, and full of fibre.

The origins of cavolo nero in the Tuscan kitchen are certainly tied to *cucina povera*, or the poor people's cuisine. Most famously, perhaps, it is one of the main ingredients in the *Ribollita* (see page 234), which would be difficult to imagine without the dark green leaves. But it has many other uses. In the province of Lucca, it is traditionally served with pork or *baccalà* (salt cod, see page 187). In Pistoia it is an essential ingredient in *Farinata* (see page 88).

The distinctive bubbly deep greenish black leaves of cavolo nero are grown extensively throughout the region. They are harvested when they are at their best after the first winter frost.

CROSTINI DI CAVOLO NERO

Cavolo nero crostini

Preparation time: 10 minutes
Cooking time: 15 minutes
Serves 6

- 4 cavolo nero cabbages, trimmed and leaves separated
- 12 slices Tuscan pane casareccio or other rustic bread
- 2 cloves garlic, peeled
- olive oil, for drizzling
- red wine vinegar, for drizzling (optional)
- salt and pepper

Bring a pan of salted water to a boil. Add the cabbage leaves and cook for 5–10 minutes, until tender.

Remove with a slotted spoon and set aside without draining thoroughly. Toast the slices of bread, rub the surfaces with the garlic cloves and put them on a serving dish.

Top each slice with the cavolo nero, letting the moisture soften the bread. Season with salt and pepper, drizzle generously with olive oil and with a few drops of vinegar, if desired.

PANCOTTO DI VIAREGGIO

Pancotto from Viareggio

In Tuscan cuisine many recipes involve lengthy cooking and 're-cooking'. The latter was once a way of avoiding any waste and using up leftovers from other meals — hence *Pappa col pomodoro* (Tomato and bread soup, see page 130), *pancotto* and *Ribollita* (see page 234).

Preparation time: 1 hour, including soaking
Cooking time: 50 minutes
Serves 6

- 8–10 slices Tuscan bread
- 200 g (7 oz) live clams
- 100 ml (scant ½ cup) olive oil
- 10 cloves garlic, peeled
- ½ dried red chilli
- 1 tablespoon tomato purée (paste)
- 175 ml (¾ cup) dry white wine
- 500 g (1 lb 2 oz) tomatoes, peeled, seeded and diced
- 400 g (14 oz) cleaned squid, cut into rings
- 1.5 litres (6 ¼ cups) fish stock
- 400 g (14 oz) uncooked prawns (shrimp), peeled and deveined
- 1 sprig flat-leaf parsley, finely chopped
- salt

Tear the bread into pieces, put it into a bowl, pour in water to cover and let soak for at least 1 hour.

Meanwhile, scrub the clams under cold running water and discard any with broken shells or that do not shut when sharply tapped with a knife. Slide the blade of a small sharp knife between the shells of a clam on the side opposite the hinge, then run the tip of the knife all the way around the shells. Run the knife around the top inside edge to separate the meat from the top shell and pull up the top shell. Run the blade around the bottom shell to separate the meat and snip off the shell. Repeat with the remaining clams.

Heat the oil in a large pan. Add the garlic cloves and chilli and cook over low heat, stirring frequently, for a few minutes, until lightly browned. Remove with a slotted spoon and discard. Mix the tomato purée (paste) with 2 tablespoons water in a small bowl and add to the pan, then pour in the wine. Increase the heat to high and bring to a boil. Add the tomatoes, clams and squid. Squeeze out the liquid from the bread, add it to the pan and mix well. Reduce the heat and simmer, stirring frequently and gradually adding the fish stock, for 30 minutes.

Add the prawns (shrimp) and parsley and cook for one more minute. Season to taste with salt and remove the pan from the heat. Serve the soup hot or warm.

FARRO AND CHESTNUT FLOUR

Farro was first cultivated by farmers in the Middle East some ten thousand years ago. It is one of the oldest forms of wheat grain and was a favoured staple of the Roman legions. Indeed, some food historians claim that the high protein and vitamin content of emmer bread and boiled grains were the key to Rome's military strength.

In Italy, the generic term *farro* includes emmer wheat, spelt and einkorn wheat. *Farro* from Garfagnana should not be confused with spelt — anyone who has cooked with both emmer wheat and spelt will know that the two are not the same and are not interchangeable. Farro has long been associated with the mountainous Garfagnana region. The combination of poor mountainous soils with environmental conditions such as climate and altitude sets the farro from Garfagnana apart from that grown anywhere else, and gives it its distinctive flavour.

Another major staple from the Garfagnana region is chestnut flour made from the sweet chestnut, not the horse chestnut. Chestnuts, known locally as *neccio*, have been cultivated here since around 1,000 AD when the trees were introduced to meet the needs of a growing population. The chestnut tree became known as the 'bread tree' and, because the chestnuts themselves were used to make flour, they became known as 'tree bread'. So important was this staple that in 1489 the city of Lucca passed special laws to protect the chestnut groves and to regulate the production of chestnut flour.

The culinary traditions associated with chestnuts have survived for the most part intact, and today chestnuts still feature strongly in the local cuisine.

The best way to enjoy fresh chestnuts as they come into season is simply to roast them over hot coals. Festivals are held throughout the area to celebrate their arrival every year.

MINESTRA GARFAGNINA DI FARRO

Garfagnina farro soup

Preparation time: 15 minutes + overnight soaking (optional)
Cooking time: 2–3¾ hours
Serves 4

- 200 g (1 cup) dried borlotti beans, soaked overnight in water to cover and drained, or 500 g (3 cups) fresh borlotti beans
- 150 ml (⅔ cup) olive oil, plus extra for drizzling
- 50 g (⅓ cup) finely chopped lardo (pork fat) or pancetta
- 2 ripe tomatoes, peeled, seeded and finely chopped
- 1 celery stalk, finely chopped
- 1 small onion, finely chopped
- 1 carrot, finely chopped
- 1 clove garlic, finely chopped
- 1 sprig sage, finely chopped
- 1 sprig rosemary, finely chopped
- 200 g (scant 1 cup) farro, rinsed
- salt and pepper

If using dried beans, put them into a large pan and pour in water to cover. Bring to a boil and boil vigorously for 15 minutes, then drain. Return the beans to the pan, pour in water to cover and bring to a boil. Reduce the heat and simmer for 1½–2 hours, until tender. If using fresh beans, bring a large pan of water to a boil, add the beans, reduce the heat and simmer for 1 hour, until tender.

Meanwhile, heat the oil in a shallow pan. Add the lardo or pancetta, tomatoes, celery, onion, carrot, garlic, sage and rosemary and cook over low heat, stirring occasionally, for 30 minutes. Season with salt and pepper.

When the beans are tender, drain them, reserving the cooking liquid. Add the beans with a little of the cooking liquid to the pan of vegetables and purée the mixture with a stick blender. Alternatively, press the beans through a sieve (sifter) before adding them to the pan.

Cook, stirring occasionally, for 5 minutes, then stir in the reserved cooking liquid and bring to a boil.

Add the farro and cook over medium heat, stirring occasionally, for about 1 hour, until tender. Taste and season with salt and pepper, then transfer the soup to a warmed tureen. Drizzle with 1–2 rings of olive oil and serve immediately.

GARMUGIA

A great deal of mystery surrounds this dish (see page 70). Some claim that the name derives from the ingredients — that is, the buds (*germogli* in Italian) of spring. The mix of fresh vegetables, which include spring onions (scallions), artichokes, asparagus tips, broad (fava) beans and peas, would certainly suggest that it was a dish cooked in the spring.

However, unlike so many of Tuscany's soups, which have their roots in *cucina povera*, the inclusion of minced (ground) beef in the recipe would suggest that this was a dish of the middle and upper classes. It is alleged to have originated in the seventeenth century and, according to the famous Tuscan writer Mario Tobino, was introduced to treat lingering winter colds amongst Lucca's middle class. Tobino is not alone in attributing therapeutic qualities to this soup and even to this day, many locals fiercely believe in the restorative value of this spring time cure.

Traditionalists argue that the best way to cook *garmugia* is on the embers of a fire. However, this age-old method has, for the most part, given way to the convenience of a low flame on the stove. Like many Tuscan soups, it is always poured into the bowl on top of toasted bread and sometimes it is served with grated Parmesan too.

Huge stacks of fresh artichokes on display in Tuscan markets herald the arrival of spring.

GARMUGIA

Garmugia

Tuscans, like all Italians, eat seasonally. Spring vegetables are always eagerly anticipated and countless methods have been devised to take full advantage of the short window in which they are available.

Preparation time: 25 minutes
Cooking time: 55 minutes
Serves 4

- 4 tablespoons olive oil
- 100 g (generous ½ cup) finely chopped lardo (pork fat), or Italian sausage, skinned and chopped
- 3 onions, thinly sliced
- 100 g (scant 1 cup) minced (ground) beef
- 100 g (¾ cup) shelled broad (fava) beans
- 150 g (1 ¼ cups) shelled peas
- 200 g (7 oz) asparagus tips
- 4 globe artichokes, trimmed and very thinly sliced
- 700 ml (3 cups) beef stock
- 8 slices toasted bread
- 2–3 tablespoons grated Parmesan cheese
- salt and pepper

Heat the oil in a flameproof casserole. Add the lardo or sausage and onions and cook over low heat, stirring occasionally, for 5 minutes, until softened. Add the minced (ground) beef and cook, stirring and breaking it up with the spoon, for 4 minutes.

Stir in the beans, peas, asparagus tips and artichokes and cook, stirring occasionally, for 15 minutes. Pour in the stock and simmer for 30 minutes. Season the soup to taste with salt and pepper and remove the pan from the heat.

Arrange the slices of toasted bread in the bottom of 4 individual soup bowls, sprinkle with the Parmesan and ladle the soup on top. Serve immediately.

ARISTA AL FINOCCHIO

Pork loin with fennel

The Greek word *aristos* translates to excellence of any kind. In 1440, a group of envoys who took part in the Ecumenical Council in Florence described the excellent pork loin they had just eaten with this adjective. The Italian word *arista*, pork loin, is said to have derived from this incident.

Preparation time: 20 minutes
Cooking time: 1 hour + 10 minutes for resting
Serves 6

- 1 × 1-kg (2¼-lb) boned and rolled loin of pork
- 65 g (generous ⅓ cup) chopped pancetta or lardo (pork fat)
- 1 clove garlic, chopped
- 1 large sprig wild fennel, chopped
- 3–4 tablespoons olive oil
- salt and pepper
- sautéed potatoes or turnips, or boiled beans, to serve

Preheat the oven to 160°C/325°F/Gas Mark 3. Using a small sharp knife make small slits all over the pork.

Mix together the pancetta or lardo, garlic and fennel and push the mixture into the slits in the pork. Heat the oil in a roasting pan, add the pork and cook over medium-high heat, turning frequently, until evenly browned. Season with salt and pepper, transfer to the oven and roast for about 1 hour, until cooked through.

Check by piercing the meat; if the juices run clear, the pork is cooked. Alternatively, it is cooked when a meat thermometer registers an internal temperature of 80°C/176°F. Remove the pan from the oven and let the pork rest for 10 minutes, then slice and serve with sautéed potatoes or turnips or boiled beans.

CROSTATA DI RICOTTA GARFAGNINA

Garfagnina ricotta tart

Ricotta, often described as a cheese, is in fact a milk product and is made using the whey, the watery liquid left over from cheesemaking. It can be made from cow, sheep or goat's whey and is at its best when eaten fresh.

Preparation time: 40 minutes
Cooking time: 1 hour + 5 minutes for resting
Serves 6

- 70 g (generous ½ cup) raisins
- 4 tablespoons Marsala
- 500 g (2 cups) ricotta
- 100 g (½ cup) caster (superfine) sugar
- 1 tablespoon plain (all-purpose) flour, plus extra for dusting
- 4 eggs, separated
- 100 ml (scant ½ cup) single (light) cream
- grated zest and strained juice of 1 lemon
- 250 g (9 oz) ready-made shortcrust pastry (basic pie dough)

Put the raisins and Marsala into a bowl and let soak for 30 minutes, until plumped up. Drain, reserving the soaking liquid.

Preheat the oven to 180°C/350°F/Gas Mark 4. Line a 26–28-cm (10½–11-inch) round cake pan with baking parchment.

Push the ricotta through a sieve (sifter) into a bowl, then beat in the sugar. Gently stir in the flour, reserved soaking liquid, egg yolks, cream, grated lemon zest and raisins until thoroughly combined. Whisk the egg whites with 1 teaspoon lemon juice in a grease-free bowl until stiff peaks form, then fold into the mixture.

Set aside a small amount of dough for the lattice. Roll out the remainder on a lightly floured surface into a round slightly larger than the prepared pan and use to line it. Spoon the ricotta mixture into the pastry case (shell). Roll out the remaining dough and cut into strips. Arrange them over the filling in a lattice pattern, brushing the edges with water to seal. Put the pan on a baking sheet and bake for 1 hour. Remove the tart from the oven, let stand for 5 minutes and serve warm.

III

PISTOIA

Pistoia draws most of its culinary inspiration from the natural resources of the Apennines. The Etruscans lived in these parts before it became a Roman colony in the sixth century BC, but the city's golden age began in 1177 when it proclaimed itself a free municipality entitled to make its own laws. However, rivalry and warfare between Italy's small city states was prolonged and commonplace, and Pistoia was no exception. Continuous fighting with its neighbour, Florence, hindered prosperity and gained Pistoia a black reputation among Florentines. Both Dante and Michelangelo commented negatively about the province, Michelangelo going so far as to call the Pistoiese 'enemies of heaven'.

Previous page:
The luscious persimmon or sharon fruit is one of the last fruits of the year and is picked from the trees in the early winter.

Peasant cooking traditions run deep in Pistoia. Foraging was always an important source of food: wild fruits from the forest were used to make a variety of jams and preserves, and mushrooms featured in many local dishes. Most important to survival, however, was the sweet chestnut which, in the absence of wheat, was ground to make flour. Every year, the villagers took part in an ancient ritual called the *Maconeccio* (*maco* meaning 'abundant' and *neccio* being local dialect for 'chestnut'). Towards dusk on 29 September, the feast of St Michael, people would congregate in their village square with torches, metal pots and pans and cowbells before setting off in procession towards the chestnut woods while crying out as loud as they could, 'Maconeccio! Maconeccio!' The noise was intended to ward off witches and evil spirits and to ensure a good harvest — which was, in former times, a matter of life or death.

Recycling, a condition born of necessity in Pistoia, has become something of a mainstay of the local cuisine. Today's famous dishes such as *Crostini rossi alla chiantigiana* (Chianti-style red crostini, see page 84) owe their origins to inventive ways of using leftovers. Another once typical dish that originated from the principle of never letting anything go to waste was *il*

Freshly picked cep (porcini) mushrooms on display in a market in Pistoia.

carcerato (literally, 'the prisoner'). It was devised by inmates at the prison of Santa Caterina in Brana, which stood on a riverbank facing a slaughterhouse. Every day, offal which was not sold was thrown into the river, and the prisoners were given permission to collect the discarded cuts which they used to create a soup. Today, a version of the dish can still be found in traditional *trattorie* in the area, albeit enriched with wild herbs, garlic and local cheese.

Pasticceria Carli in Lamporecchio has been making traditional wafer biscuits (cookies) known as *brigidini di Lamporecchio* on waffle irons since the early nineteenth century. Folklore has it that the biscuits were invented by chance in the sixteenth century when the nuns at the convent in Lamporecchio got the mix wrong when preparing the Host for Sunday Mass. It could no longer be used at the Mass, but rather than wasting it, they added anise seeds to make biscuits.

Finally, brief mention must be made of the *birignoccoluti* of Pistoia, more commonly known as *confetti* (sugared almonds). This local speciality is recorded as having been eaten at a feast on 25 July 1372 to celebrate the patron saint of the city. The *confetti* of Pistoia are easily differentiated from those made elsewhere because of their irregular and lumpy shape. Since the 1960s it has been traditional for a newly married couple to present their wedding guests with a *bomboniera*, a lace bag containing five *confetti*: one each for health, wealth, happiness, fertility and longevity.

SORANA BEANS

Behind every typical Tuscan product there is a story, and so it is with the humble sorana bean. They were requested by Rossini, composer of the famous operas *The Barber of Seville* and *William Tell*, in lieu of payment for the revision of a friend's musical scores, so it is hard to imagine that not too long ago this bean was facing extinction. The mass exodus of workers from the Pistoian countryside after the Second World War was such that by the early 1980s only one producer remained, faithfully cultivating the bean that had for centuries been the staple of the Tuscan countryside. But with the recent revival of interest in Tuscan country cuisine, the sorana bean's special culinary properties have been rediscovered.

Today there are some twenty producers in an area of hardly more than 10 hectares (25 acres) along the banks of the Pescia river. The land here consists of rich alluvial soil, known as *ghiareto*, from the flood waters. Everything about the sorana bean is steeped in tradition and myth. Sowing can only take place during the last moon of May and on the days of the week which do not contain an 'r' (which in Italian means Sunday, Monday, Thursday and Saturday). Once harvested, the beans are left out to dry for several days before being carefully packaged along with grains of pepper and sometimes laurel leaves to keep weevils away. Both the bags and bottles of beans are then wax-sealed to confirm their authenticity.

PECORINO CHEESE

The cheesemakers of Pistoia still make their cheese by a centuries-old traditional method, and this is what makes their product so special. The native sheep are the Massese, a wild breed with gunmetal-coloured fleece, dark spiral-shaped horns and bulging bright eyes. They are raised on mountain pastures during the milder months and taken into the fold over the winter. A mere twenty cheesemakers in the area still follow what can be a gruelling regimented process, which often begins with milking the sheep by hand. Only natural rennet is used and, most importantly, the milk is never pasteurized, a rare practice today in Tuscany.

Three main types of cheese are produced: *formaggio fresco*, a fresh cheese; *abbucciato,* a semi-fresh cheese which takes approximately a month to mature; and pecorino, which is allowed to mature for three months to one year. All three cheeses are round, with the fresh and semi-fresh ones weighing about 1 – 1.5 kg (2¼ – 3¼ lb) and the pecorino weighing up to 3 kg (6½ lb). Also produced from the same milk are the *Raviggiolo* (see page 230) and ricotta cheeses which must be eaten within one or two days.

A tray of Pecorino cheeses at various stages of maturity. Pecorino cheese, which is made from sheep's milk, is the most popular and widely available of all cheeses produced in the region.

CROSTINI ROSSI ALLA CHIANTIGIANA

Chianti-style red crostini

There are countless recipes for Tuscan crostini which, although fairly similar, vary according to the cook's taste. Some use *pane casareccio*, plain rustic bread, others use typical unsalted Tuscan bread baguettes. Some leave the bread plain, others toast it, fry it in oil or soak it in stock. In the latter case the rule is that, if the bread is toasted, the stock must be hot and vice versa. The slice should be dampened only on the spreading side. Other variations concern the addition of aromatic herbs to the tomato mixture but this is all a matter of taste.

Preparation time: 25 minutes
Serves 4

- 200 g (7 oz) wholemeal (whole wheat) bread
- 4 tablespoons white wine vinegar
- 2 large ripe tomatoes, peeled, seeded and chopped
- 1 tablespoon capers, drained, rinsed and chopped
- 3 tablespoons chopped flat-leaf parsley
- 2 tablespoons chopped thyme
- 1 clove garlic, chopped
- 3 tablespoons olive oil
- 8 slices Tuscan bread, toasted, or pan-fried polenta
- coarse salt and pepper

Tear the bread into pieces and put them into a bowl. Pour in the vinegar and let soak for 5 minutes, then drain and squeeze out well. Transfer to a mortar or another bowl, add the tomatoes, capers, parsley, thyme, garlic and oil and season with salt and pepper. Pound with a pestle or the end of a rolling pin to form a coarse mixture. Spread the mixture on slices of toasted bread or pan-fried polenta and serve.

SALVIA FRITTA IN PASTELLA

Sage fried in batter

One of the region's favourite herbs, *salvia* (sage) has been used in Tuscan cooking since at least the fifteenth century. In the Tuscan kitchen it is used constantly: it is added to stews or sauces for pasta, sautéed with potatoes, cooked with chickpeas or beans, or simply sautéed until crisp and eaten with meat. This recipe dating from the Renaissance was originally made with salted anchovies that had been soaked in milk to remove the salt.

Preparation time: 25 minutes
Cooking time: 15 minutes
Serves 5

— 100 g (scant 1 cup) plain (all-purpose) flour
— 1 egg
— 200 ml (scant 1 cup) iced water
— salt
— anchovy paste, for spreading
— 20 large sage leaves
— vegetable oil, for deep-frying

To make the batter, sift the flour with a pinch of salt into a bowl and make a well in the centre. Add the egg to the well and beat incorporating the flour gradually with a balloon whisk or wooden spoon. Gradually whisk in the iced water until smooth.

Spread a little anchovy paste on 1 side of each sage leaf and sandwich them together in pairs. Heat the oil in a deep-fryer to 180–190°C/350–375°F or until a cube of day-old bread browns in 30 seconds. Using tongs, dip the leaves in the batter, shake off the excess and add to the hot oil in batches. Cook for a few minutes, until light golden brown. Remove with a slotted spoon, drain on paper towels and serve hot.

FARINATA

Farinata

Preparation time: 10 minutes + overnight soaking
Cooking time: 3½ hours
Serves 6

- 250 g (scant 1½ cups) dried borlotti beans, soaked overnight in water to cover and drained
- 2 cloves garlic, peeled
- 2 sage leaves
- 100 g (3½ oz) cavolo nero cabbage
- 4 tablespoons olive oil
- 1 carrot, chopped
- ½ celery stalk, chopped
- ½ onion, thinly sliced
- 2 large ripe tomatoes, peeled, seeded and chopped
- 150 g (1 cup) polenta
- 4 tablespoons grated pecorino cheese
- salt and pepper

Put the beans into a large pan and pour in water to cover. Bring to a boil and boil vigorously for 15 minutes, then drain and return to the pan. Add 1 garlic clove and the sage, pour in 2 litres (8¾ cups) water and bring to a boil. Reduce the heat and simmer for 1½–2 hours, until tender, seasoning with salt towards the end of the cooking time.

Meanwhile, bring a pan of lightly salted water to a boil. Add the cabbage and simmer for 5 minutes, then drain and chop.

When the beans are tender remove the pan from the heat. Remove and discard the sage and garlic. Drain, reserving the cooking liquid, and press half the beans through a sieve (sifter) into a bowl.

Chop the remaining garlic. Heat the olive oil in a large pan. Add the carrot, celery, onion, tomatoes and second clove of garlic and cook over low heat, stirring occasionally, for 10 minutes, until softened. Stir in 400 ml (1¾ cups) of the reserved cooking liquid, the bean purée, the remaining whole beans and the cabbage. Simmer for 30 minutes.

Pour 1 litre (4¼ cups) of the remaining reserved cooking liquid into the pan, season with salt and pepper and sprinkle in the polenta. Cook, stirring constantly and adding more cooking liquid or water if necessary, for 40 minutes, until thickened and cooked through. Stir in the pecorino, ladle into individual serving bowls and serve immediately. The farinata is also excellent served cold.

POLLO FRITTO IN PASTELLA

Deep-fried chicken in batter

Preparation time: 30 minutes + 1 hour for resting
Cooking time: 40 minutes
Serves 6

For the batter:

- 400 g (3 ½ cups) plain (all-purpose) flour
- 3 eggs, separated
- 50 ml (¼ cup) dry white wine
- 1 tablespoon olive oil
- grated zest and strained juice of ½ lemon
- salt and pepper

- 1 ½ × 1.5-kg (3 ½-lb) chickens
- vegetable oil, for deep-frying
- 2 lemons, sliced

First, make the batter. Sift the flour with a pinch of salt into a bowl and make a well in the centre. Add the egg yolks, wine and oil to the well and beat with a balloon whisk or wooden spoon until smooth. Gradually beat in enough water to make a soft batter. Season with pepper, stir in the lemon zest, cover and let rest for at least 1 hour.

Meanwhile, cut the chickens into small pieces and carefully remove the bones and skin.

Whisk the egg whites with 1 teaspoon lemon juice in a grease-free bowl until stiff peaks form. Gently fold them into the batter. Heat the vegetable oil in a deep-fryer to 180–190°C / 350–375°F or until a cube of day-old bread browns in 30 seconds. Working in batches, add a few pieces of chicken to the batter, turning to coat, then remove with a slotted spoon, draining off the excess. Add them to the hot oil and cook until golden brown all over. Remove with tongs, drain on paper towels and keep warm while you prepare and cook the remaining batches. Transfer to a warmed serving dish, garnish with the lemon slices and serve immediately.

CASTAGNACCIO

Castagnaccio (chestnut cake, see page 95) is a typical Tuscan dessert made with chestnut flour. It goes by many names, including *migliaccio*, *baldino* (in Arezzo), *pattona* (in Livorno), *ghiriglio* (found in parts of the Florentine countryside) and *ghirighio* (in Prato).

Brown in colour, it is firm in texture with a soft centre and should be consumed fresh, at most three days after making it. It is not a cake in the sense of 'sponge' cake, but more like a dense chestnut purée (almost like a baked cheesecake in texture).

The traditional version of *castagnaccio*, known as the poor man's cake, was very different from its modern-day equivalent. It would have been much heavier and not sweet, designed more to fill the stomach than to please the palate. Today, the inclusion of raisins, pine nuts and sometimes sugar has broadened its appeal. Many Tuscan families still make *castagnaccio* at home, but it can also be found in bakeries and pastry shops throughout Tuscany in the autumn (fall) and winter, after the annual production of chestnut flour. It is best enjoyed thinly sliced and is often accompanied with ricotta or mascarpone cheese and a glass of wine.

In the mountainous regions, the chestnut was the most precious of all produce. Eaten fresh or dried, ground to make flour or boiled, it provided an essential source of food all year round.

CASTAGNACCIO ALLA PISTOIESE

Pistoian-style chestnut cake

The best chestnut flour for this recipe comes from Monte Amiata. Always store chestnut flour in the refrigerator.

Preparation time: 20 minutes
Cooking time: 40 minutes
Serves 6–8

- 50 g (scant ½ cup) raisins
- 3 tablespoons olive oil, plus extra for brushing
- 600 g (5 ¼ cups) very fresh chestnut flour
- 1 teaspoon salt
- 100 g (scant 1 cup) pine nuts
- 100 g (scant 1 cup) shelled walnuts, coarsely chopped
- 1 small sprig rosemary

Put the raisins into a bowl, pour in warm water to cover and let soak for 15 minutes, until plumped up. Drain, squeeze out the excess liquid and pat dry with paper towels.

Preheat the oven to 220°C/425°F/Gas Mark 7. Brush a 30-cm (12-inch) round cake pan with about 3 tablespoons oil.

Sift the chestnut flour into a bowl and gradually stir in about 900 ml (3¾ cups) water to make a smooth batter. Stir in the salt, pine nuts and raisins and mix well. Pour the mixture into the prepared pan and sprinkle with the walnuts and a few rosemary needles.

Drizzle with the oil, put the pan on a baking sheet and bake for 40 minutes, until the top is golden and the surface is cracked. Remove the pan from the oven and let cool slightly, then serve.

IV

PRATO

The province of Prato was established on 16 April 1992, making it Tuscany's newest region. However, the food traditions of Prato, as might be expected, predate this event by many hundreds of years. In fact, there are historical documents dated as early as 804 AD which show wine and oil production in the area.

Previous page:
Dedicated to *Santo Stefano* (Saint Stephen), the earliest records of the cathedral in Prato date back to the tenth century. The *campanile* (bell tower) was completed in the fourteenth century.

This, the smallest Tuscan province, is situated in the northeast of the region between the provinces of Pistoia and Florence. The city of Prato lies to the south of the mouth of the Bisenzio valley, which, carrying the river of the same name, runs the length of the province. To the east of the city are the Calvana Mountains — a series of high, bare-topped hills — and to the west the Monteferrato Hills. This wide range of terrain has given rise to a distinct and varied cuisine, albeit with a strong Tuscan flavour. Sheep's milk cheeses from the Calvana Mountains, chestnuts from the upper Bisenzio valley, cured meats from the Prato plains and wines from Carmignano are prime examples of the wonderful flavours to be found in this area.

Like most Tuscan cuisine, the food of Prato today is very much a descendant of *cucina povera*, typified by the two local staples: *bozza* bread and celery. *Bozza* bread is the pride of the bakers of Prato. The locals will tell you that its lack of salt makes it easier to match the bread with different accompaniments, both savoury and sweet. The first documented reference to the *bozza* of Prato was in the sixteenth century, by which time it was already being sold on Florentine market stalls where it was held in high esteem. The people of Prato still have *bozza* bread every day. When fresh it is often eaten with the local *mortadella* (spiced pork sausage), and when stale, as nothing ever goes to waste, it is used for such Tuscan staples as *Pappa col pomodoro* (Tomato and bread soup, see page 130).

Sedano alla pratese (Prato-style celery, see page 104) is also a dish that originated during hard times. Rather than throwing out the tough outer stalks of a bunch of celery, housewives from Prato devised a dish that would transform them into something delicious. The stalks were stuffed with either chicken livers or *mortadella di Prato*, eggs and Parmesan cheese, rolled in flour, coated in egg and sautéed. The dish was traditionally cooked for the festival of the *Madonna della Fiera* in September, and is still served in restaurants in Prato today.

Moving south of the city of Prato to the Carmignano region, *amaretti di Carmignano* (a type of almond macaroon) are a local speciality for those with a sweet tooth. The original recipe dates back to the nineteenth century and was devised, it is claimed, by one Giovanni Bellini, known also as *I'Fochi* (the fiery one) because of his notorious temper. The area also produces *fichi secchi di Carmignano* (dried figs), from the *dottato* variety of fig. At harvest time, the fresh figs are eaten either with *mortadella di Prato* or stuffed with cream cheese and pine nuts.

In a region well-known for its wines, those of Carmignano deserve mention. Wines have been produced in the area since Roman times. In 1716 Carmignano wines were selected by Cosimo III de' Medici to be included among four areas of superior wine production, making them among the first wines in Italy to be given protected status, long before more famous Tuscan wines such as Chianti.

In the Val Tiberina, *friggione del contadino* or 'farmer's fry-up' is a typical dish for using up leftovers. The women of the house were skilful and creative in this art in the days when the frugal habit of not wasting anything was still widespread.

LESSO RIFATTO CON PATATE

Boiled meat hash with potatoes

Preparation time: 20 minutes
Cooking time: 50 minutes
Serves 4

- 3 tablespoons olive oil
- 1 onion, finely chopped
- 500 g (3 ½ cups) boiled meat, cut into small pieces
- 500 g (1 lb 2 oz) boiled potatoes, sliced
- 3–4 sage leaves or 1 sprig rosemary
- 500 g (1 lb 2 oz) tomatoes, peeled, seeded and diced
- salt and pepper

Heat the oil in a large, shallow pan. Add the onion and cook over low heat, stirring occasionally, for 5 minutes, until softened. Add the meat, increase the heat to medium and cook, stirring frequently, for 5 minutes, until lightly browned. Using a slotted spoon, remove the meat from the pan, set aside and keep warm.

Add the potatoes and sage or rosemary to the pan and mix well, then stir in the tomatoes and season with salt and pepper. Reduce the heat and cook for 5 minutes.

Return the meat to the pan and simmer for another 15–20 minutes, until thickened and piping hot. Serve immediately.

MORTADELLA

Mortadella di Prato is a cooked pork salami that was first made in Prato in the early 1900s. As with many Tuscan specialities, frugality played a significant part in its early history. It was initially conceived as a convenient way of using up leftovers and lesser cuts of meat that were not considered good enough for the preparation of more prestigious salami such as *finocchiona*. A particularly heady concoction of spices and a sweet liqueur known as Alchermes was therefore mixed with the meat, apparently to mask undesirable flavours.

Today, thankfully, salami-makers no longer feel the need to mask the flavour of their mortadella. That is because the meats now used in its production are carefully selected and include a mix of choice lean cuts from the shoulder as well as fat from the cheeks and back. Alchermes is still used to colour the sausage and as a flavouring, along with a mix of herbs and spices which include pepper, cinnamon, garlic, cloves and coriander. It comes in various shapes, generally similar to either the classic salami or wider like the classic mortadella depending on the producer, and is normally about a kilo (just over 2 lb) in weight. If you are lucky enough to be passing a *salumificio* (salami-maker's shop) just as the mortadella has been cooked, it is delicious warm. But it is also excellent eaten the more usual way, thinly sliced and accompanied by *bozza* bread and figs from Carmignano.

Finocchiona, a sausage flavoured with wild fennel seeds is a true Tuscan delicacy. The aging process lasts between five months to a year.

SEDANO ALLA PRATESE

Prato-style celery

Preparation time: 1 hour
Cooking time: 30–40 minutes
Serves 4

- 8 large celery stalks, trimmed
- 50 g (4 tablespoons) butter
- 1 small onion, chopped
- 75 g (¾ cup) mortadella or chicken livers, chopped
- 125 g (generous 1 cup) minced (ground) veal
- 3 eggs
- 80 g (⅔ cup) grated Parmesan cheese
- 4 tablespoons plain (all-purpose) flour, for dusting
- olive oil, for frying
- 400 g (1¾ cups) leftover meat ragù
- salt and pepper

Cut the celery into 8-cm (3-inch) lengths. Bring a pan of salted water to a boil, add the celery and blanch for 5 minutes. Drain well, then refresh in a bowl of cold water. Wrap the pieces in a clean dish towel and weigh down with a weight, such as 2 or 3 cans of tomatoes, to extract as much liquid as possible.

Meanwhile, melt the butter in a frying pan or skillet. Add the onion and cook over low heat, stirring occasionally, for 10–15 minutes, until softened. Add the mortadella or chicken livers and veal and cook, stirring frequently, for 10 minutes.

Mix together 1 egg and the Parmesan in a bowl and season with salt and pepper. When the meat is cooked, add this mixture to the pan and stir well, then remove from the heat. Stuff a piece of celery with the meat mixture, cover with another piece of celery, press together and tie with string. Continue in this way until all the ingredients have been used.

Spread out the flour in a shallow dish and beat the remaining eggs in another shallow dish. Roll the stuffed celery in the flour, then dip in the beaten eggs.

Pour olive oil into a frying pan or skillet to the depth of 1 cm (½ inch) and heat. Add the stuffed celery, in batches if necessary, and cook until golden. Remove with a slotted spoon and set aside. Heat the ragù in a pan, adding a little extra water or stock, if necessary. Add the celery and simmer gently for 20–30 minutes, until it has thickened and is tender. Transfer to a warmed serving dish and untie before serving.

CAVOLFIORE IN UMIDO

Stewed cauliflower

There are two varieties of cauliflower cultivated in Tuscany, harvested from November through to April. The *precoce toscano* is harvested at the beginning of the season and the *fiorentino tardivo* is a late harvesting variety. Cauliflower is always boiled first in the Tuscan kitchen, before being incorporated into other dishes or having other flavours added.

Preparation time: 30 minutes
Cooking time: 1½ hours
Serves 4

- 1 cauliflower, trimmed and cored
- 3–4 tablespoons olive oil
- 1 clove garlic, peeled
- 1 tablespoon tomato purée (paste)
- 150 ml (⅔ cup) hot vegetable stock
- salt and pepper

Bring a large pan of lightly salted water to the boil. Add the cauliflower and cook for 25–30 minutes, until tender. Drain well, then break into florets and thinly slice them vertically.

Heat the oil in a shallow pan. Add the garlic clove and cook for a few minutes, until golden brown. Remove with a slotted spoon and discard. Add the cauliflower and cook over low heat, gently turning the slices, for a few minutes, until lightly browned. Season with salt and pepper. Mix the tomato purée (paste) with the hot stock in a small bowl and stir it into the pan. Cover and simmer gently, adding more liquid if necessary, for 1 hour. Remove from the heat, transfer to a warmed serving dish and serve immediately.

CANTUCCI

It is hard to imagine a more fitting finale to a Tuscan meal — especially if you happen to be in Prato — than a glass of Vin Santo and a cantucci biscuit (cookie). The biscuits of Prato, popularly known as *Cantucci* or *Cantuccini* (see page 115), are made from flour, eggs, sugar, toasted almonds and pine nuts. The mix is rolled into logs, flattened, baked, allowed to cool and then sliced diagonally. Some bakeries will then bake them again to dry and crispen them, though others maintain that this is not necessary. The most important thing is to achieve the right consistency, crunchiness and flavour. These qualities enable the biscuit to perform its main function, which is to be dipped into a glass of Vin Santo: the biscuit soaks up the flavour of the wine and in return the wine softens the outside of the biscuit, which remains dry and crunchy on the inside to create a contrast of textures to complement the flavours.

The origins of these biscuits date back to 1858 when Antonio Mattei opened the doors of his small artisan *biscottificio* (biscuit shop) at No.22 Via Ricasoli. The sign above the shop, which still exists today, says it all: 'Antonio Mattei, Fabricante di Cantucci'. In honour of their inventor the biscuits are affectionately known by the locals as *mattonelle*, and more than 150 years since the little shop in Via Ricasoli first opened they are still prepared to the same traditional recipe. Today, few visitors to Prato leave without at least one of the distinctive blue waxed-paper packets of Antonio Mattei's celebrated cantucci.

CHOCOLATE VALLEY

Tuscany's food and wine heritage is undisputed: centuries-old artisanal traditions have secured the region a prime place on the world's gastronomic map. Producers of superlative Tuscan wines, cheese, olive oil and cured meats hardly need an introduction, but today there is another speciality that is fast becoming synonymous with trademark Tuscan quality, and few would guess what it is: chocolate.

A quiet revolution has been taking place behind closed doors in unassuming Tuscan farmhouses. So successful has it been that today the Valdinievole and the surrounding area, along a line connecting Prato and Pistoia and stretching down to the northern reaches of Pisa, has been dubbed the 'Chocolate Valley'. The roots of the revolution stretch back to the mid-1970s when Roberto Catinari, a native of Pistoia, returned home after twenty years studying and working with Swiss chocolatiers. He set to work, applying his knowledge of chocolate to the flavours of the Tuscan landscape. His chocolate, which sold from a small shop in the town of Agliana, was an instant success and others quickly followed his example.

In just a few decades, the success of Tuscan chocolate has been remarkable. Chocolate Valley is now home to some of the most acclaimed chocolatiers in the world — from the originator, Catinari in Agliana to Amedei in Pontedra, de Bondt in Pisa, Mannori in Prato and Slitti in Monsummano. Together they have established a centre of excellence that rivals their closest competitor Piedmont, not to mention the traditional leaders in the field, the Swiss and the Belgians.

Following pages:
(Page 110) Dutch born Paul de Bondt, artisan chocolatier, is now a full-time resident in the Chocolate Valley, at work in his laboratory near Pisa.

(Page 111) A selection of the creative chocolate bars made by de Bondt, which include combinations such as plain chocolate with lemon zest, orange peel or dried pears, or milk chocolate and dried figs.

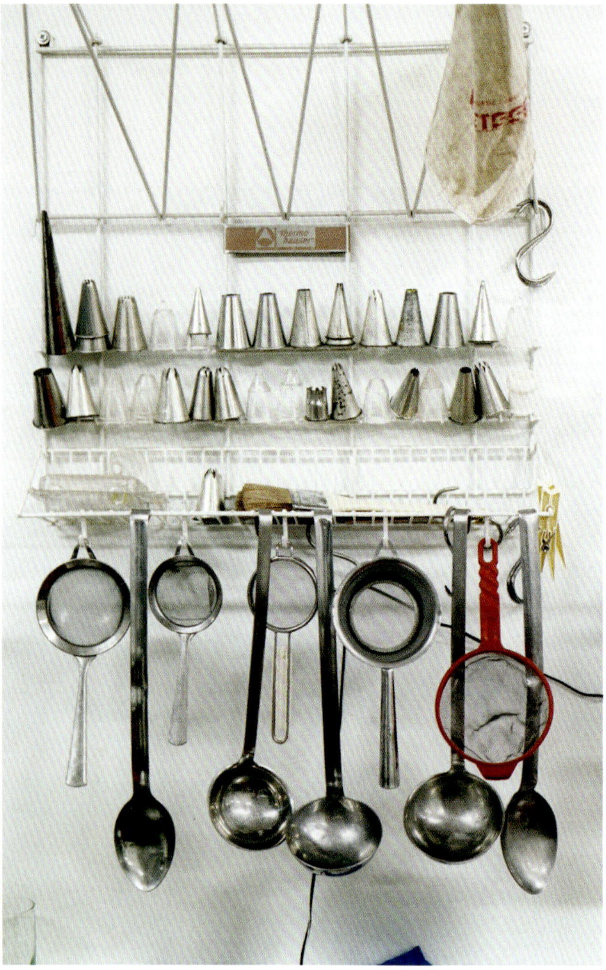

PREMIATO
A
FIRENZE
1861
LONDRA
ANTON
FABBRICA

MATTEI
DI CANTUCCI
COTTI
ALTRI
PARIGI
1867
FIRENZE
1870
20

VIN SANTO

CANTUCCI

Cantucci

Traditionally, these biscuits (cookies) have always been made with unpeeled almonds. Some recipes, including the original Mattei recipe, include 20 grams (¼ cup) of finely chopped pine nuts, which lend a slightly different texture to the finished biscuits. True *cantucci* were made with bread dough, sugar, anise seeds and oil.

Preparation time: 30 minutes
Cooking time: 30 minutes
Serves 4

- butter, for greasing
- 500 g (4 ½ cups) all-purpose flour, plus extra for dusting
- 500 g (2 ½ cups) caster (superfine) sugar
- 1 teaspoon baking powder
- 3 eggs
- 2 egg yolks
- pinch of saffron threads, crushed
- 250 g (2 ¼ cups) shelled almonds, in their skins
- salt

Preheat the oven to 160°C/325°F/Gas Mark 3. Grease and flour 2 baking sheets.

Sift the flour, sugar, baking powder and a pinch of salt into a mound on a work surface (counter) and make a well in the centre. Break 2 eggs into the well and add the egg yolks and saffron. Gradually incorporate the dry ingredients with your fingers. Add the almonds and mix well.

With floured hands, take small pieces at a time and shape into long rolls, 2–3 cm (1¼–1¾ inches) wide and 1 cm (½ inch) thick. Put the rolls on the prepared baking sheets. Lightly beat the remaining egg in a small bowl and brush the tops of the biscuits. Bake for 30 minutes. Remove from the oven, cut into 3–4 cm (1¼–1½ inch) pieces at an angle. When completely cool, store in an airtight container.

Previous page:
Birthplace of the *cantucci*, the Antonio Mattei shop in Prato still produces its biscuits using the original recipe from 1858.

ZUPPA INGLESE CON SPUMONI AL CARAMELLO

Custard with caramel meringue

Preparation time: 40 minutes
Cooking time: 45 minutes
Serves 6

For the custard:

- 1 litre (4 ¼ cups) milk
- thinly pared strip of lemon zest
- 4 egg yolks
- 4 tablespoons caster (superfine) sugar
- 1 tablespoon cornflour (cornstarch)

- 100 g (3 ½ oz) sponge (lady) fingers
- 120 ml (½ cup) freshly brewed coffee, cooled
- 4 tablespoons brandy
- 4 egg whites
- 4 tablespoons caster (superfine) sugar
- 50 (¼ cup) granulated sugar

To make the custard, pour the milk into a pan, add the lemon zest and bring just to a boil, then remove from the heat and set aside. Beat the egg yolks with the sugar in a bowl until light and fluffy. Gently fold in the cornflour (cornstarch). Remove and discard the lemon zest from the milk and stir the milk into the mixture. Pour the custard back into the pan and cook over low heat, constantly stirring, for about 20 minutes, or until the custard coats the back of the spoon.

Remove from the heat and set aside, stirring occasionally to prevent a skin from forming.

Put the sponge (lady) fingers in a shallow dish in a single layer. Mix together the coffee and brandy in a bowl and pour the mixture over the sponge fingers.

Arrange the sponge fingers in layers in a dessert bowl, pour the custard over them and let stand in a cool place.

Whisk the egg whites with the caster (superfine) sugar in a grease-free bowl until stiff peaks form. Put the granulated sugar into a heavy shallow pan and stir in 1 tablespoon water. Heat the mixture gently until it turns a pale caramel colour, then remove from the heat and pour steadily over the egg whites, whisking constantly until thoroughly combined. Spoon the mixture over the custard and serve.

Previous page:
Vin Santo (holy wine) is the classic Tuscan amber-coloured dessert wine. It is traditionally made from Trebbiano and Malvasia grapes, which are left to dry to concentrate the sugars.

RISTORANTE
PIZZERIA
Lo Scudo
PIZZ

V

FLORENCE

First-time visitors often remark how quickly they feel at home in Florence. That is because it is one of those few cities that most people have known second-hand all their lives. Whether it's patting the head of the bronze boar, window shopping for jewellery along the Ponte Vecchio, admiring the splendours of Piazza del Duomo or gazing up at Michelangelo's *David*, the rituals of a visit to Florence are well and truly rehearsed.

Previous page:
Designed by Arnolfo Di Cambio in 1367, the distinctive dome of the Duomo in Florence was achieved by the architectural and engineering brilliance of Filippo Brunelleschi who commenced work on the dome almost a century later in 1420.

Florence, provincial capital and the capital of Tuscany itself, is the region's most populous city. Lying on the banks of the river Arno, it is widely considered the birthplace of the Renaissance and one of the most beautiful cities in the world. It has also been the home of many of Italy's most influential thinkers, artists, and writers, including Leonardo Da Vinci, Machiavelli, Dante, Michelangelo, Galileo, Botticelli and Pellegrino Artusi, author of the most influential cookbook in Italian history, *La scienza in cucina e l'arte di mangiar bene (Science in the Kitchen and the Art of Eating Well)*, published in 1891.

Another famous Florentine was Catherine de' Medici, who married Henry II of France in 1533. For some time it was believed that Catherine was responsible for importing Italian (or, rather, Florentine) cuisine to France and thereby civilizing the French table. But the story has no basis in fact. One of the dishes she is said to have brought with her was *cibreo* (cock's comb), an ancient recipe for *rigaglie* (dish with offal and assorted bits and pieces of fowl) cooked in wine along with onions, garlic and butter. The dish is finished with lemon juice and a beaten egg. Whether Catherine did or did not bring this dish to France is a matter of debate. What can, however, be said with certainty is that the dish does have Florentine origins, and it is one that epitomizes the Florentine preoccupation with all things offal-related. In another dish, *Fegatelli* (Livers, see page 263), the livers are skewered along with bay leaves and pieces of stale bread and cooked over an open fire. The most famous offal dishes are the many

The distinctive evergreen cypress tree is as much an integral part of the Tuscan landscape as the olive tree. Very long-lived, some trees are reported to be more than 1,000 years old.

Vines are harmoniously blended into every curve, every turn of the Tuscan hillside. They are fundamental to the Tuscan way of life.

based on tripe, sold from mobile stalls throughout the city.

Catherine's story does draw attention to one further facet of Florentine cuisine that should not be overlooked. Throughout the Renaissance, Florence was a city of considerable wealth — in fact, much of Tuscany's riches were concentrated there. So, unlike other parts of Tuscany where the cuisine has evolved largely from peasant traditions, Florentine cooking is a hybrid of *cucina povera* and the food of the wealthier class. Florence's best-known dish, for example, *Bistecca alla fiorentina* (Florentine-style steak, see page 136) was for long beyond the reach of all but the privileged few.

For most of the population, the staples of beans, bread and other assorted vegetables were the norm. To this end, the best place to see what the province of Florence has to offer is the city's markets, and in particular, the Mercato di Sant'Ambrogio and the San Lorenzo market in the city centre. The majority of Florentines still flock to the markets to buy their food, many preferring to go daily, so that everything is as fresh as possible. The range of locally grown produce is impressive and includes the delicately flavoured Empoli artichokes, *certaldo* onions, used to make a kind of jam which is eaten with local cheeses; and *mugello,* sweet chestnuts which were granted PGI (Protected Geographic Indication) status by the EU in 1996. At the Friday market, *baccalà* (salt cod, see page 187) is always on offer. One of the most commonly used fish in Florentine cuisine, it is sometimes boiled or sautéed, but most typically cooked with tomatoes, in dishes known as *alla fiorentina*, or Florentine-style.

Following page:
The *Ponte Vecchio* in Florence crosses the river Arno at its narrowest point. Dating back to Roman times, the bridge is today home to an array of jewelry and antique shops.

After doing their shopping, Florentines might pause to regroup over espresso and something sweet, or perhaps a *negroni*, a heady cocktail of Campari, gin and red vermouth. There are few better places to sample a *negroni* than Caffè Giacosa, opened in 1815, where Florence's famous cocktail is claimed to have originated. Caffè Giacosa is also famed for its sweets, pastries and chocolates. In fact, there are any number of venues throughout Florence that will please even the most discerning chocoholic. At Hemingway's, in the Piazza Piattellina, every conceivable chocolate treat is on offer, as well as chocolates from some of Tuscany's most acclaimed producers. Caffè Rivoire on the Piazza della Signoria came to fame with its delectable *cioccolato caldo* (hot chocolate), and its range of chocolates and pastries is not to be neglected either. Wherever you go in Florence, telltale signs of the city's latest renaissance (the chocolate one) are seldom far away.

TOMATOES

Tomatoes were introduced to Italy in the sixteenth century, although they were not used in cooking until some time later. Nowadays, with eleven varieties grown in the area, Tuscans are spoilt for choice. Among their favourites is the big, pulpy *pomodoro costoluto fiorentino*, which is great eaten fresh or used to make *passata* (puréed tomatoes). Also popular in Florentine vegetable gardens is the *pomodorino da inverno da appendere* (a type of winter cherry tomato for hanging). The plant produces clusters of six to eight tomatoes which are smooth, slightly elongated and pointed. They are kept hanging in ventilated rooms during the winter, meaning that good-quality fresh tomatoes can be eaten almost all year round.

Arguably the most famous Tuscan dish that uses tomatoes is *Pappa col pomodoro* (Tomato and bread soup, see page 130). The word *pappa* refers to mushy baby foods, and the dish takes its name from its texture.

With over ten traditional locally grown varieties of tomato, it is hardly surprising to find that this fruit features strongly in all areas of Tuscan cuisine.

PAPPA COL POMODORO

Tomato and bread soup

This very tasty, yet simple tomato-based soup is known throughout Italy, and was made famous in the 1960s by Rita Pavone's song '*Viva la pappa col pomodoro*' (Long Live Pappa col Pomodoro). Although some purists will argue that to make a true *pappa col pomodoro* you need to use Tuscan unsalted bread and Tuscan extra-virgin olive oil, the main thing is to ensure that you use a good rustic country loaf and, of course, the highest-quality tomatoes at the peak of their season. There are endless variations, and because it can be reheated and eaten hot, cold or tepid, it is also one of the region's most versatile dishes. It almost certainly originated in the countryside and is a true legacy of *cucina povera* — another example of the region's many inventive ways of using up leftover bread.

Preparation time: 15 minutes
Cooking time: 15 minutes
Serves 6

- 500 g (1 lb 2 oz) tomatoes, peeled, seeded and coarsely chopped
- 6 cloves garlic, peeled
- 10 basil leaves
- 5 tablespoons olive oil, plus extra for drizzling
- 6 slices day-old or toasted bread
- salt and pepper

Press the tomatoes through a sieve (sifter) into a bowl. Pour 1.5 litres (6¼ cups) water into a large pan, add the garlic cloves, basil leaves, oil and a pinch each of salt and pepper. Bring to a boil over medium heat and add the tomatoes. Reduce the heat and simmer for 10–15 minutes.

Remove and discard the garlic cloves and basil leaves. Put the slices of bread in a tureen and gradually pour the tomato mixture over them. Let stand for a few minutes, then drizzle with 2 rings of olive oil and serve.

PEPOSO

Peposo

The *fornacini* (those who worked on the furnaces for making terracotta tiles) cooked *peposo* in a pan brought from home in the great heat given off by the furnaces, adding a generous amount of pepper.

Preparation time: 20 minutes
Cooking time: 5 hours
Serves 6

- 1 kg (2 ¼ lb) stewing beef, cut into cubes
- 3 garlic cloves, peeled
- 1 heaped tablespoon freshly ground black pepper
- 1 tablespoon tomato purée (paste)
- 350 ml (1 ½ cups) red wine
- salt
- boiled potatoes, polenta or toast, to serve

Put the meat into a terracotta pot or flameproof casserole, add the garlic and pour in water to cover.

Half cover the pot or casserole and cook over medium heat for 2 hours. Stir in the pepper, tomato purée (paste) and wine, season with salt, cover and simmer for another 3 hours, until thick and creamy. If the stew seems to be drying out, add a little hot water. Serve hot with boiled potatoes, polenta or toast.

Previous page:
A view of Palazzo Serristori along the banks of the river Arno. Built in the sixteenth century the palazzo is now home to a papal school.

FLORENTINE-STYLE STEAK

The *Bistecca alla fiorentina* (Florentine-style steak, see page 138), as the name implies, has always been a Florentine dish, though beyond the reach of all but the wealthy. Indeed, such was the demand amongst the elite that the butchers of Siena would send to Florence only the expensive rear quarters of the animal (from which the steak is obtained), keeping the more popular fore quarters for themselves.

Florentines take their steaks very seriously. In 1991 representatives of the Florentine Butchers' Association through the Association of the Florentine T-bone Steak Academy set guidelines for the selection and cooking of a *fiorentina*. A proper T-bone steak must be cut from the loin through the fillet and the sirloin with the T-bone in the middle. It must be between 3 and 4 centimeters (1¼ and 1½ inches) thick and have broad dimensions.

In restaurants it is usually priced by the *etto* (100 g/ 3½ oz) and a large steak can be very expensive. Often, because of both the cost and the size, a steak will be shared by two or more people. Many Florentines say that a genuine *Bistecca alla fiorentina* must be meat from Chianina cattle (see page 251), an indigenous breed from the Val di Chiana. However, the truth is that today demand outstrips supply, so restaurants serve T-bones from Argentina, Brazil and France. Chianina steaks are rarely available, and when they are they cost considerably more. However, if you do manage to find them and you want the real thing it is well worth the extra expense.

A Florentine steak must be marbled with fat so as to keep it moist during cooking.

BISTECCA ALLA FIORENTINA

Florentine-style steak

Few dishes better symbolize Florence and evoke a sense of place than *Bistecca alla fiorentina*. Known abroad as either a T-bone or porterhouse steak, to the Florentines it is simply a *bistecca* and was originally known as *carbonata*. The word *bistecca* comes from the English word beefsteak. The term gained currency in the mid-nineteenth century with the arrival of British settlers in Tuscany.

Preparation time: 5 minutes
Cooking time: 10 minutes
Serves 4

- 2 × 600-g (1 lb 5-oz) steaks
- olive oil, for drizzling
- salt and pepper

Preheat the grill (broiler). Add the steaks and grill (broil) for 5 minutes on each side, until browned on the outside and just pink inside. Remove from the heat and sprinkle with salt. Drizzle a ring of oil on a warmed serving dish, put the steaks on it and serve immediately, sprinkled with pepper.

TRIPE

The tradition of eating tripe (*trippa*), is more deeply rooted in Florence than anywhere else in Italy. At lunchtime, come rain or shine, Florentines gather around mobile tripe stands where *trippai* (tripe vendors) dish out small plastic tubs or *panini* (sandwiches) packed with slices of tripe cooked in any number of ways. Featuring daily on the menu is *Trippa alla fiorentina* (Florentine-style tripe, see page 142), tripe stewed in wine with tomatoes, celery, carrots, onions and spices and topped with a good grating of parmesan cheese. Most popular, perhaps, is a peasant dish made with the fourth stomach of the veal, sliced into strips, loaded into a *panino* (sandwich), and finished with a pinch of salt and a squeeze of *salsa piccante* (chilli sauce). There are many other variations on the theme. In Livorno, generous amounts of garlic and parsley are added; in Montalcino the tripe is cooked in wine, and in Siena it is cooked with sausage.

Tripe is the term generally used for a cow's stomach. Ruminants have, however, multiple stomachs and in Italy, the various 'tripes' take on different names according to their origin. *Croce* (smooth white tripe), the most common tripe, is the first of the three fore-stomachs of the animal. It is followed by *cuffia* (spongy honeycomb tripe) and *centopelli*, which is typically used to prepare a highly flavoured soup. Finally comes the tender *lampredotto*, which is from the actual stomach and darker in colour.

Florentines, more than most, understand and appreciate the nutritional and gastronomic value of this part of the animal, and do not consider it an inferior cut of meat. Cooked properly, tripe is a healthy dish, simple and honest yet utterly delicious.

Once considered poor man's fare, tripe is now a gastronomic delicacy. When properly prepared, tripe is delicious and flavourful as it soaks up the rich juices of a sauce.

TRIPPA ALLA FIORENTINA

Florentine-style tripe

Tripe in Italy is always sold fully pre-cooked. In other countries you need to check with your butcher to see how much it has been pre-cooked and vary your cooking time accordingly. Perfectly cooked tripe should be slightly chewy but always tender.

Preparation time: 30 minutes
Cooking time: 1 hour 40 minutes
Serves 4

- 800 g (1 ¾ lb) precooked tripe
- 5 tablespoons olive oil
- 1 clove garlic
- 1 celery stalk, finely chopped
- 1 carrot, finely chopped
- 1 onion, finely chopped
- 4 basil leaves, finely chopped
- 175 ml (¾ cup) dry white wine
- 80 g (1 cup) grated Parmesan cheese
- 400 g (14 oz) tomatoes, peeled, seeded and chopped
- salt and pepper

Bring a large pan of salted water to a boil and cook the tripe for 20 minutes, then drain and plunge into a bowl of cold water.

Meanwhile, heat the oil in a flameproof casserole. Add the garlic clove and cook over low heat for a few minutes, until golden, then remove with a slotted spoon and discard. Add the celery, carrot, onion and basil and cook over very low heat, stirring occasionally, for 20 minutes, until lightly browned. Add the wine and cook until the alcohol has evaporated.

Drain the tripe thoroughly and cut it into strips, then add it to the casserole. Sprinkle with half the Parmesan cheese and mix well, then stir in the tomatoes and season with salt and pepper. Simmer gently, adding a little hot water if the mixture begins to dry out, for 30–40 minutes.

Remove the casserole from the heat, transfer the tripe and sauce to a warmed serving dish and serve immediately. If desired, sprinkle with Parmesan.

ZUCCOTTO

Zuccotto

According to legend, *zuccotto* is the first *semifreddo* (an Italian frozen dessert) in the history of cooking and was originally made in an infantryman's studded helmet. In the Tuscan dialect *zucca* means 'head'. It was originally prepared with ricotta, glacé (candied) fruit, almonds and dark (semisweet) chocolate.

Preparation time: 30 minutes + 6 hours for freezing
Cooking time: none
Serves 6

- 1 × 250–300-g (9–11-oz) pan di Spagna or Madeira cake
- 120 ml (½ cup) amaretto liqueur
- 500 ml (generous 2 cups) double (heavy) cream
- 80 g (scant ½ cup) caster (superfine) sugar
- 50 g (½ cup) unsweetened cocoa powder
- 4 amaretti biscuits (cookies)

Line a freezerproof semi-circular mould with clingfilm (plastic wrap). Cut the cake horizontally into 2 rounds of equal thickness. Divide 1 of the rounds into 8 wedges and use to line the the bottom and sides of the mould. Mix the liqueur with a little water and sprinkle it over the cake slices.

Whisk the cream in a bowl, gradually adding the sugar, until stiff peaks form. Spoon one-third of the cream into another bowl and fold in half the unsweetened cocoa powder. Crumble the amaretti into the remaining cream and spoon into the mould, gently spreading it over the side and leaving a small hollow in the centre. Spoon the cocoa cream into the hollow and smooth the surface. Put the remaining cake round on top, cover and freeze for at least 6 hours.

Turn out the zuccotto onto a serving dish and remove and discard the clingfilm. Put the remaining unsweetened cocoa powder into a small sieve (sifter), sprinkle it over the dessert and serve immediately.

CHIANTI

In terms of fame, few could dispute that Chianti is the king of Tuscan wines. The region lays claim to some of the oldest wine traditions in Italy, even in Europe. At its best it can produce wines to rival anything that is made in Piedmont. But beyond these broad generalizations, Chianti is a wine about which there is confusion and misunderstanding.

The Sangiovese grape is the cornerstone of Tuscan Chianti. The *vendemmia* (grape harvest) takes place in September and festivals are held throughout the region to celebrate this most important occasion.

Part of the problem lies in the name. 'Chianti', as a generic label, can be used to indicate wines from the provinces of Pisa, Lucca, Arezzo, Pistoia, Prato, Florence and Siena. The wines produced in this area are still associated in many minds with the straw-covered flasks of cheap wine that were once ubiquitous in pizzerias and trattorias throughout the world. However, times have changed, and today there are many good Chiantis, just as there are many ordinary ones.

Wines labelled Chianti Classico DOCG are those produced in the original Chianti zone in the hills between Florence and Siena, and bear the traditional symbol of the *gallo nero* (black cockerel) on a pink label. The label is a badge of distinction, designed to differentiate Chianti Classico from the wares of the army of producers who have been entitled to assume the name 'Chianti' since 1932 when new regulations resulted in the enlargement of the production zone. It is claimed that the label's origins lie in the ancient rivalry between Florence and Siena.

The story goes that in 1208 the Florentines and Sienese agreed on a somewhat unusual means of settling their border dispute. At cockcrow on a chosen morning, two horsemen would ride out with all speed from their respective cities, and the border would be designated at the point at which they met. But the tale has it that the Florentines cheated, riding further than the Sienese because they starved their cockerel so that

Following page:
A landscape spectacular in every season, the Tuscan hills turn gold and red as the leaves from the vines begin falling in the approach to winter.

it would crow before dawn, thereby gaining a time advantage.

As with all Chianti, the grape of choice is Sangiovese, often in combination with small amounts of Canaiolo, Cabernet Sauvignon and other grapes. The recent trend is towards darker, richer, more structured, firmer wines. Given the number of producers in the area, an exhaustive list would be impossible. Moreover, it would be incomplete as some of the most established and reputed producers in the area have opted out of membership of the *consorzio*, the consortium of wine producers.

However, with these qualifications in mind, notable producers include Ama, Antinori, Bossio, Capaccia, Casaloste, Collelungo, Colombia di Cencio, Casa Emma, Fonterutoli, Fontodi, Isole E Olena, La Massa, Monsanto, Palazzino, Querciabella, Rampolla, Ricasoli, Ruffino, San Felice, San Giusto, Villa Cafaggio and Volpaia. The best way to find a good producer of Chianti Classico is undoubtedly to buy a couple of bottles and find a style that you like. It is hard to imagine a better way of doing this than a leisurely drive along the Strada Chiantigiana, the Chianti Route, where visitors to Chianti Classico producers are always welcome.

An *enoteca* (local wine bar) showcases the best of local wines the region has to offer.

CastelGiocondo
LE DIFESE
IL BRUCIATO
ENOTECA
TOGNON

FRUTTA SCELTA
FRUTTA SCELTA

VI

PISA

In the north-west of the city of Pisa is a group of buildings which attracts tourists from all over the world. Whatever time of day you visit, the Piazza dei Miracoli, commonly known as the Piazza del Duomo, is crowded with coachloads of visitors who have come to see the famous Campanile — better known as the Leaning Tower of Pisa. But Pisa is much more than an architectural miscalculation which has turned into a tourist honeypot.

Previous page:
Courgette (zucchini) flowers, considered a delicacy, must be eaten as soon as possible after picking to best appreciate their delicate flavour.

The province of Pisa stretches from the coast down into central Tuscany, a landscape dominated by gently rolling hills dotted with farms. The city of Pisa lies in the north of the province, just inland from the coast and close to the vast National Park of Migliarino San Rossore. And, as might be expected, the produce from this area is remarkable in its richness and variety.

The province is a fertile and unpolluted land of vineyards, olive groves, orchards and fields devoted to vegetables. The pine nuts from the National Park of Migliarino San Rossore and the white truffles of San Miniato in the north are its most famed culinary products. Shops in San Miniato proudly display a staggering range of truffle products, from truffle-flavoured sausages and salami to truffle oils and butters, truffles in jars and even truffle-flavoured chocolates. But there's much more on offer than truffles: San Miniato also offers an abundance of gastronomic delights such as porcini mushrooms, chestnuts and honey.

Other produce from the area includes the San Miniato artichoke, considered one of the world's tastiest varieties and used in the kitchens of the Medici during the Renaissance. Also widely cultivated are the *pisanello* and *costoluto fiorentino* tomato varieties, the Tuscan cauliflower and the *mora* courgette (zucchini), noted for its flower which is particularly resistant to wilting. In markets throughout Tuscany, courgettes are sold with their flowers attached: the flowers are stuffed and

Courgettes (zucchini) are a popular vegetable eaten and grown throughout the region. They are generally picked and eaten when young, tender and slim.

deep-fried while the courgettes themselves are commonly added to soups.

Cured pork products such as salami and pancetta are popular in the province. Also highly prized is the *soppressata di sangue* from Pisa, a boiled black pudding (blood sausage) made from a combination of lean and fatty cuts. This sausage, made all over the province of Pisa, is eaten sliced, floured and sautéed in oil or reheated in boiling water and served as a side dish. Another local speciality is *fegatello di maiale macinato pisano* (Pisan minced [ground] pork liver). Meat from the neck, leg and liver is minced, mixed with wild fennel, wrapped in nets and cooked in clay pots with lard. Once cooked, it is preserved in more lard and eaten typically within a week. It is easy to see why this was traditionally regarded as a substantial and nourishing winter dish.

In addition to pine nuts, the park of Migliarino San Rossore is also noted for its lamb. The semi-wild sheep of the Massese breed are fed on hay, fresh forage and grains; their meat has a sweet, delicate flavour. The park is also home to small game such as hare, rabbits and pheasant, all of which feature strongly in the local cuisine.

Despite such a short coastline, fish features strongly in Pisan cuisine. In part, this reflects its past as a small maritime republic before Italy was united as a single country in the nineteenth century. One of its most famed specialities was a dish made with baby eels fished from the mouth of the river Arno. The fish were sautéed quickly in oil with sage, and lemon juice and Parmesan added at the last minute. As it is now prohibited to fish for baby eels, today the dish is prepared with whitebait. Other notable Pisan fish dishes include grilled mullet from the mouth of the river Arno and a poached spotted weever. Dried cod cooked with leeks or chickpeas or in a sweet and sour sauce is also popular.

Pancetta (cured belly of pork) can take two forms, *tesa* (flat) or *arrotolata* (rolled). In the rolled version the meat is spiced, tied into a cylindrical shape and hung to age.

WHITE TRUFFLES FROM SAN MINIATO

There is an old folk saying, still recounted to the children of San Miniato and the surrounding countryside, that there is a little golden calf to be found somewhere between the towns of Doderi, Montoderi and Poggioderi. It is hardly a coincidence that the area, known as the Valdegola triangle, is also the heart of Tuscany's best-known truffle-hunting ground. There may or may not be a golden calf buried somewhere in the vicinity, but there are certainly white truffles — if your dog has a good nose and you know where to look.

White truffles are a type of fungus. They differ from black truffles in that they are rarer, more difficult to find and cannot be farmed. Thus, the white truffle is generally considered superior. The edible fruiting body normally grows to between 3 and 16 centimetres (1–6 inches) in size, resembles a knobbly potato and is creamy in colour. It has been referred to as the 'white diamond of the kitchen'.

In Italy, white truffles are normally associated with Alba in Piedmont. Yet, as truffle hunters in San Miniato point out, these are the same genus of truffle, *Tuber Magnatum Pico*, as are found in the province of Pisa. They may also mention that the largest white truffle ever found, weighing 2,520 grams (5 lb 10 oz), was unearthed in 1954 by a *tartufaio* (truffle hunter) from the village of Balconevisi in San Miniato.

Every year, in the last three weeks of November, the area's most precious commodity is honoured at the internationally recognised *mostra mercato nazionale del tartufo bianco di San Miniato* (The San Miniato National White Truffle Market), during which time the city is transformed into an open air gastronomic celebration.

As leaves turn russet red and gold across the countryside, the start of the white truffle hunting season is signaled.

FRITTATINE IN TRIPPA

Frittata 'tripe'

This faux 'tripe' is a popular Tuscan recipe. In another version of this dish the strips of frittata are cooked in *lardo* (cured pork back fat), chopped onion, marjoram and wine and then finished with a generous sprinkling of pecorino cheese.

Preparation time: 5 – 10 minutes
Cooking time: 20 minutes
Serves 6

- 6 eggs
- 2 tablespoons olive oil, plus extra for drizzling
- 1 clove garlic, peeled
- 120 ml (½ cup) tomato sauce
- 40 g (½ cup) grated Parmesan cheese
- 6 slices toasted bread (optional)
- salt

Lightly beat the eggs with a pinch of salt in a bowl. Drizzle a little olive oil into a frying pan or skillet and heat. Pour in the beaten eggs and cook over low heat for 1 – 2 minutes, until the eggs start to set. Shake the pan gently to loosen the frittata, then cover the pan with a flat plate and, holding it tightly, invert the pan. Slide the frittata back into the pan and cook the second side for 2 – 3 minutes, until golden brown.

Remove the pan from the heat, turn the frittata on to a chopping (cutting) board, roll it up and cut into strips. Heat the oil in a shallow pan. Add the garlic clove and cook over low heat for a few minutes, until golden. Remove with a slotted spoon and discard. Add the tomato sauce and simmer for 10 minutes, then stir in the strips of frittata. Sprinkle with the Parmesan, cover and cook for another 2 – 3 minutes.

Transfer to a warmed serving dish, garnish with the slices of hot toasted bread and serve immediately.

FARAONA AI PORCINI

Guinea fowl with porcini

Guinea fowl meat has a more pronounced flavour than that of chicken. It is extremely popular throughout the country, not just for its flavour but also its versatility, as it lends itself to a number of ways of cooking. It can be roasted simply or stuffed and roasted, cut into small pieces and pan fried or stewed.

Preparation time: 20 minutes
Cooking time: 55 minutes
Serves 4

- 1 guinea fowl, cut into 4 pieces
- 8 small sprigs sage
- 8 small sprigs mint
- 4 slices pancetta
- 6 tablespoons olive oil
- 2 garlic cloves, peeled
- 400 g (generous 5 ½ cups) porcini mushrooms, sliced
- 4 mint leaves
- 3 ripe tomatoes, chopped
- salt and pepper

Preheat the oven to 180°C/350°F/Gas Mark 4. Stud the pieces of guinea fowl with the sage and mint sprigs and arrange a pancetta slice over each. Pour 4 tablespoons of the olive oil into a casserole and add the guinea fowl. Roast in the oven for 35 minutes.

Meanwhile, heat the remaining oil in a shallow pan with the garlic cloves. When the garlic begins to brown, remove with a slotted spoon and discard. Add the mushrooms, mint leaves and tomatoes to the pan and cook over low heat, stirring occasionally, for 10 minutes.

Remove the guinea fowl from the oven, add the pieces to the pan with the mushrooms and cook for 15 minutes. Season with salt and pepper and remove the pan from the heat. Transfer the guinea fowl and mushrooms to a serving dish and serve immediately.

Following page:
Poultry such as chickens, ducks, geese and turkeys are still an important source of food for Tuscan families in the countryside.

POLLO AL SUGO CON I 'ROCCHINI'

Chicken in sauce with rocchini

Preparation time: 25 minutes
Cooking time: 1 hour 20 minutes
Serves 4–6

- 3–4 tablespoons olive oil
- 1 carrot, finely chopped
- 1 red onion, finely chopped
- 1 clove garlic, finely chopped
- 1 celery stalk, finely chopped
- 1 sprig flat-leaf parsley, finely chopped
- 1 sprig thyme, finely chopped
- 1 sprig basil, finely chopped
- 1 × 1.5–2-kg (3¼–4½-lb) chicken, cut into pieces
- 175 ml (¾ cup) red wine
- 1 tablespoon tomato purée (paste) or 6 tomatoes (some unripe), peeled, seeded and diced
- salt and pepper

For the rocchini:

- 1 head celery, coarse stalks removed
- plain (all-purpose) flour, for dusting
- 2 eggs
- vegetable oil, for deep-frying
- grated Parmesan cheese, for sprinkling
- salt

Heat the oil in a large, shallow pan. Add the carrot, onion, garlic, celery, parsley, thyme and basil and cook over low heat, stirring occasionally, for 5 minutes, until softened. Add the pieces of chicken, increase the heat to medium and cook, turning frequently, for 10–15 minutes, until evenly browned. Season with salt and pepper, pour in the wine and cook until the alcohol has evaporated. If using tomato purée (paste), mix it with 175 ml (¾ cup) warm water and stir it into the pan. If using fresh tomatoes, stir them into the pan. Reduce the heat, cover and simmer for 30 minutes, until the chicken is tender and cooked through. Test by piercing the thickest part; if the juices run clear, the chicken is ready.

To make the rocchini, bring a pan of salted water to a boil and cut the tender celery stalks into 10-cm (4-inch) lengths. Add the celery to the pan and simmer for 15–20 minutes, then drain and mash into a paste. Form into balls. Spread out the flour in a shallow dish and beat the eggs with a pinch of salt in another dish. Heat the vegetable oil in a deep-fryer to 180–190°C/350–375°F or until a cube of day-old bread browns in 30 seconds. Dip the celery paste balls first in the flour and then into the beaten egg. Add them to the hot oil, in batches and cook until golden brown. Remove with a slotted spoon and drain on paper towels.

Transfer the chicken pieces to a warmed serving dish and add a few spoonfuls of the sauce. Add the rocchini to the remaining sauce and cook for a few minutes, until softened. Sprinkle with the Parmesan, transfer to the serving dish and serve immediately.

PINE NUTS

Pinoli, as the Italians call pine nuts, are the seeds of *Pinus pinea*, the Mediterranean stone pine tree, which grows throughout central and southern Italy. Their culinary use dates back to Roman times. The pine nuts of the Migliarino San Rossore National Park are certified as organic and are produced throughout the whole area. Annual production is about 2,000 tons and the harvesting process is long and laborious, a fact which is reflected in the price. First the pine cones are gathered, spread out on sheets and left to dry, which can take up to seven months. The seeds or nuts are then separated from the cones and the shells removed, and only after drying are they finally ready for use.

In Italy pine nuts are sold in small packets, or loose by the *etto* (100 g/3½ oz) at the market. About 6 mm (¼ inch) long and cream in colour, they have a texture and consistency entirely their own. The flavour, mild and slightly resinous, works well in both savoury and sweet dishes. Pine nuts are commonly added to meat and game dishes, particularly those that are cooked in an *agrodolce* (sweet-sour) sauce. They also add texture to pasta sauces and are used in baked goods.

PISAN DESSERTS

Pine nuts feature heavily in the cakes of the region, one of the most popular being *Torta della nonna* (Grandmother's torte, see page 172). The widely known *Torta della nonna* holds a special place in the hearts and imagination of Italians. It is now a fixture throughout Italy, and every family has its own opinion on how it is best made. Despite its popularity, the cake's origins remain shrouded in mystery because no reliable documentation has been found to explain it. All that is known is that the two basic ingredients *pasta frolla* (shortcrust pastry or basic pie dough) and *crema pasticceria* (confectioner's custard), became fashionable in European kitchens during the Renaissance in the sixteenth century. At some stage, someone must have had the idea of combining them. And just to complicate matters, some food historians claim that the cake was originally made with ricotta, rather than *crema pasticceria*. If this is the case, the cake may well have been a descendant of a Roman dish.

Pine nuts also feature in the popular *Torta pisana* (Pisan torte, see page 170) and the *Torta coi bischeri*. The latter has been made in the area since the eleventh century and takes its name from the little rolls of pastry arranged around the cake which resemble the small peg used to adjust the strings on a violin called a *bischero*. At the Nuova Artigiana Dolci cake shop on Via Vittorio Veneto in Pontasserchio, the town where the cake originated, it is still made to the traditional recipe which is strictly protected by the local council.

Whenever or wherever its origins, its importance for most Italians lies in its association with *cucina della nonna* (grandmother's cooking). In Tuscany and throughout Italy it is family food, born behind closed doors. Today, practically every restaurant, trattoria and pasticceria in Tuscany serves *torta della nonna* and it is as popular now as it has ever been — whenever that was.

TORTA PISANA

Pisan torte

Preparation time: 30 minutes
Cooking time: 50 minutes
Serves 6

- 120 g (½ cup) butter, softened, plus extra for greasing
- 350 g (3 cups) self-raising flour, plus extra for dusting
- 1 teaspoon vanilla sugar
- 1 teaspoon baking powder
- 275 g (scant 1½ cups) caster (superfine) sugar
- 2 large (US extra large) eggs, separated
- 4 tablespoons milk
- 1 teaspoon lemon juice
- 150 g (1¼ cups) pine nuts

Preheat the oven to 180°C/350°F/Gas Mark 4. Line the bottom and sides of a 24–26-cm/9½–10½-inch tart pan with baking parchment. Grease the sides of the pan with butter and sprinkle with flour, tipping out any excess. Sift together the flour, vanilla sugar and baking powder into a bowl.

Put the butter and 250 g (1¼ cups) of the sugar into another bowl and beat until pale and fluffy. Add the egg yolks, 1 at a time, and continue to beat until foamy. Gradually stir in the flour mixture, alternating it with spoonfuls of milk. Whisk the egg whites with the lemon juice in a grease-free bowl until stiff peaks form, then gently fold into the mixture.

Pour the mixture into the prepared pan and sprinkle with the pine nuts and remaining sugar. Bake for 50 minutes. Remove the pan from the oven, put it on a wire rack and let cool completely before turning out and serving.

TORTA DELLA NONNA

Grandmother's torte

Preparation time: 20 minutes
Cooking time: 1 hour
Serves 8

For the pastry (pie) dough:

- 300 g (2 ¾ cups) plain (all-purpose) flour, plus extra for dusting
- 80 g (scant ½ cup) caster (superfine) sugar
- 1 teaspoon baking powder
- 150 g (⅔ cup) butter, cut into pieces, plus extra for greasing
- 1 egg
- 1 egg yolk
- grated zest of 1 lemon
- salt

For the filling:

- 500 ml milk
- thinly pared strip of lemon zest
- 3 egg yolks
- 120 g (scant ⅔ cup) caster (superfine) sugar
- 50 g (½ cup) plain (all-purpose) flour
- pinch of vanilla powder or a few drops vanilla extract

To decorate:

- 1 egg, lightly beaten
- chopped almonds and/or pine nuts, for sprinkling
- icing (confectioners') sugar, sifted

To make the dough, sift together the flour, sugar, baking powder and a pinch of salt into a mound on a work surface (counter) and make a well in the centre. Add the butter, egg, egg yolk and lemon zest and gradually incorporate the dry ingredients using your fingers. Mix well and knead lightly. Divide the dough into 2 pieces, 1 slightly larger than the other. Shape each into a ball, wrap in clingfilm (plastic wrap) and let rest in the refrigerator.

Meanwhile, make the filling. Pour the milk into a pan, add the lemon zest and bring just to a boil, then remove from the heat and set aside. Beat the egg yolks with the sugar in a bowl until pale and fluffy. Gently fold in the flour and vanilla, add the milk, combine thoroughly and pour back into the pan. Cook over low heat, stirring constantly, until the mixture coats the back of the spoon. Remove from the heat and let cool, stirring occasionally to prevent a skin from forming.

Preheat the oven to 180°C/350°F/Gas Mark 4. Grease a 24-cm (9½-inch) round cake pan with butter. Roll out the larger piece of dough on a lightly floured surface into a round slightly larger than the prepared cake pan. Ease it into the pan, leaving an overhang. Spoon the filling into the pastry. Fold the overhanging dough onto the outer edge of the case and brush with beaten egg. Roll out the other piece of dough into a round to fit the pan. Put it on top of the filling and seal the edges well. Brush the surface with the beaten egg and sprinkle with almonds and/or pine nuts in patterns. Bake for 40 minutes, until golden brown in colour. Remove the cake from the oven and let cool slightly. Remove from the pan and dust with icing (confectioners') sugar. Serve hot or lukewarm.

VII

LIVORNO

The cuisine of Livorno is a colourful amalgam of the influences of history, different cultures and territory. Originally a small fishing village on the Ligurian coast, Livorno came to prominence under the rule of the Florentine Medici family with the construction of a harbour in 1571. Livorno's position was consolidated under Ferdinand I, grand duke of Tuscany from 1587 to 1609, who declared Livorno a *porto franco*, which meant that goods traded here were duty-free. In addition, the so-called *Leggi Livornine* (Livorno Laws) accorded freedom of religion and asylum status to refugees. Within a few years Livorno was transformed into a cosmopolitan city and one of the most important trading ports in the Mediterranean. Many foreigners moved here, some to trade and some to escape religious persecution.

The legacy of Livorno's history can still be felt in its cuisine. Naturally, since it is on the coast, there is heavy reliance on a broad range of fish such as anchovies, sardines, crab, squid, octopus, clams, mussels and tuna. The Jewish population introduced tomatoes to the city and this is evident in the city's most famous dish, *Cacciucco alla livornese* (Livornese-style cacciucco, see page 182).

Of course, with a heavy concentration of asylum-seekers living in the city, poverty and wealth resided side by side. It would be difficult to imagine a dish that better reflects the reality for some, free from romantic idealizations of country cuisine, than *brodo di sassi* (rock broth), described as 'the poorest of them all'. Spongy sedimentary rocks known as *pancina livornese* were harvested from the seabed and boiled in seawater along with a few vegetables to make a broth. The liquid was then carefully strained to remove grit and sand, and *pastina* (small pasta) added to make a *minestra* (pasta soup). The dish was finished with a traditional drizzle of olive oil. At the other extreme, wealthy households, like those of the city's merchants produced dishes such as weaver fish and Livorno-style oysters.

Although the area was known predominantly for its seafood, more traditional Tuscan flavours were also incorporated into the local cuisine. *Ceci* (chickpeas) featured strongly in popular dishes such as the chickpea cake *Cecina* (see page 190) and chestnuts were evident in the local version of *castagnaccio* (see page 92), called *pattona* in Livorno. Also typical of the area was the *gallina livornese*, an Italian breed of chicken known today throughout the world, which took its name from the provincial capital. In English-speaking countries it is known as the Leghorn, after the old anglicized name for Livorno. It was exported to the USA at the beginning of the 1800s and to Britain some fifty years later. Reared in country farmyards, the *gallina livornese* was an important source of income for families as well as supplying food. One of these hens will lay up to three-hundred white-shelled eggs in a year, so it is hardly surprising that the breed was highly prized.

Following page:
Areas along the coast are framed by Mediterranean scrub. Typical plants include aromatics such as rosemary, thyme, sage and oregano, which grow wild across the region.

CACCIUCCO

This dish is Tuscany's version of the ubiquitous Italian fish soup. Its origins are uncertain, although the name is thought to have derived from the Turkish word *küçük* (which means tiny), referring to the small fish used in its preparation. One story has it that the dish came about following the death of a local fisherman who was caught in a hailstorm at sea. To prevent his family starving, each of his fellow fishermen gave the widow a piece of whatever fish they had, which she then put in a pot to make soup. Slices of stale bread accompanied it to soak up all the liquid. Passers-by, enticed by the aroma, asked how it was made, and from this the *cacciucco* was born.

Another theory has it that *cacciucco* is a reflection of the city's multi-stranded origins. From North African to Arabian and Far Eastern, from Jewish to Catholic and Muslim, the dish is said to be a culinary representation of the merging of Livorno's varied cultures, religions and traditions.

What is certain is that traditionally *cacciucco* was a dish of the poor and it was made with leftovers or lesser valued fish. There are many versions of *cacciucco*, but within the province of Livorno the dish must be spelt with five 'c's. The people of Livorno will tell you that if you see on a menu *cacciucco* spelt with only four 'c's (as other versions outside the province often are) it is best avoided, as the dish will not be typical and there won't even be a Livornese cook preparing the dish! *Cacciucco alla livornese* (Livornese-style cacciucco, see page 182) was traditionally made with at least thirteen types of fish and heavily spiced with garlic and *peperoncino* (chilli) — today, there are versions made with as few as five different varieties. It is often served poured over a slice of toasted bread rubbed with garlic, washed down with plenty of young red wine. No true Livornian would ever dream of drinking white wine with *cacciucco*.

The Tyrrhenian Sea and the Livornese coastline offer an abundance of varied and fresh seafood, which is most famously represented in Livorno's fish stew.

PRODOTTO:
€ 10,00 il Kg
Provenienza:
PESCATO LOCALE
PRODOTTO:
TRIGLIA ROSSA
Provenienza:
PESCATO LOCALE

CACCIUCCO ALLA LIVORNESE

Livornese-style cacciucco

Preparation time: 1 hour
Cooking time: 1 hour
Serves 6

- 275 ml (generous 1 cup) olive oil
- 5 garlic cloves, peeled
- 6 sage leaves
- 1 dried red chilli
- 800 g (1 ¾ lb) cleaned octopus, cut into pieces
- 700 g (1 ½ lb) cleaned mixed squid and cuttlefish, halved if large
- 450 g (1 lb) huss or shark fillet, thickly sliced
- 275 ml (generous 1 cup) red wine
- 2 ½ tablespoons tomato purée (paste)
- 1 celery stalk, chopped
- 300 g (11 oz) scorpion fish, cleaned and cut into chunks
- 700 g (1 ½ lb) tomatoes, peeled, seeded and diced
- 450 g (1 lb) large and medium uncooked prawns (shrimp) peeled and deveined
- 12 slices Tuscan bread

Heat half the oil in a large, shallow pan. Add 3 of the garlic cloves, the sage and chilli and cook, stirring frequently, for a few minutes, until the garlic is golden. Remove the flavourings with a slotted spoon and discard.

Add the octopus, squid and cuttlefish and cook for 3 minutes, then add the huss or shark and cook for another 3 minutes. Pour in the wine. Mix the tomato purée (paste) with 175 ml (¾ cup) water in a small bowl, then stir into the pan. Simmer gently for 30 minutes.

Chop 1 of the remaining garlic cloves. Heat the remaining oil in a medium pan. Add the celery and chopped garlic to the pan and cook over low heat, stirring occasionally, for 5 minutes. Add the scorpion fish and tomatoes, pour in 3–4 tablespoons water and simmer gently for 20 minutes.

Transfer the contents of the smaller pan into the larger pan and check whether the fish is cooked. Add the prawns (shrimp) and cook for 2–3 minutes, then remove the pan from the heat.

Toast the slices of bread on both sides, rub them with the remaining garlic clove and put them all around the edge of a warmed serving dish. Ladle the stew into the centre and serve immediately. You could also put the bread into 6 individual bowls, ladle the stew on top and serve.

GAMBERI IN DOLCEFORTE

Sweet and sour prawns (shrimp)

The *dolceforte* (sweet and sour) method of cooking was popular in the Renaissance in the sixteenth century. Traditionally it was a sauce that would have been made from grated chocolate, pieces of glacé fruit, cinnamon, raisins, pine nuts and sugar, to accompany game such as hare or wild boar.

Preparation time: 30 minutes
Cooking time: 10 minutes
Serves 4–6

- 100 g (¾ cup) raisins
- 1 kg (2 ¼ lb) uncooked prawns (shrimp), peeled and deveined
- plain (all-purpose) flour, for dusting
- 4 - 5 teaspoons olive oil
- ½ teaspoon ground cinnamon (optional)
- juice of 1 lemon, strained
- salt and pepper

Put the raisins into a bowl, pour in water to cover and let soak. Dust the prawns (shrimp) with flour, shaking off the excess. Heat the oil in a shallow pan. Add the prawns and cook over medium heat, stirring and turning occasionally, for 2 minutes. Season with salt and pepper and sprinkle with the cinnamon, if using. Remove from the pan and set aside.

Drain the raisins and squeeze out the excess moisture, then add them to the pan. Stir in the lemon juice and cook, stirring, until the pan juices have thickened.

Return the prawns to the pan, turn them over gently in the sauce and remove from the heat. Transfer to a warmed serving dish and serve immediately.

BACCALÀ

Baccalà (salt cod) and *stoccafisso* (air-dried cod) are popular throughout Tuscany. The two differ in the methods used to preserve the fish. For *stoccafisso* the cod is dried on sticks, sometimes on the fishing boat immediately after being caught. It is believed that the name derives from the old Dutch word *stokvish*, which means 'fish stick' or 'dried on a stick'. For *baccalà* the cod (*merluzzo*) is preserved in salt. The name originates from the Spanish for cod, *bacalao*. It is believed that Basque fishermen, who hunted whales in the open sea near Newfoundland from the 1400s, knew that the only way to preserve cod on board was to place it in salt. The method soon became widespread throughout Europe.

Before using, *baccalà* needs to be soaked in water for between twelve to forty-eight hours depending on the size and thickness of the fish. If you are buying *baccalà,* select a piece of fish that is uniform in thickness so that it soaks evenly. It should be rinsed beforehand to remove excess salt, and the water needs to be changed regularly. Too much soaking and the fish can become mushy and lose its texture; too little and it can be excessively salty and stringy.

Traditionally, pre-soaked salt cod was widely available at markets on Fridays in observance of the Catholic Church's dietary laws (Catholics are called to abstain from eating meat on Fridays in honour of the Passion of Jesus).

Baccalà (salt cod) is popular throughout Tuscany. The preserving method gives it its unique flavour and even when fresh fish is available many Italians will still opt for salt cod.

BACCALÀ CON LE CIPOLLE

Salt cod with onions

At the time of the first press of wine, or during the olive harvest, rural workers in the Maremma area (which begins south of Livorno and forms a coastal plain running to the very southern end of Tuscany) took grilled (broiled) salt cod with them as a snack.

Preparation time: 30 minutes + soaking time
Cooking time: 45 minutes
Serves 6

- 1.2-kg (2 ½ lb) salt cod, soaked in several changes of water for 12 – 48 hours and drained
- plain (all-purpose) flour, for dusting
- 150 ml (⅔ cup) olive oil
- 2 garlic cloves, peeled
- 1 large white onion, thinly sliced
- 800 g (1 ¾ lb) ripe tomatoes, peeled seeded and diced
- 2 tablespoons chopped flat-leaf parsley (optional)
- salt and pepper

Pat the fish dry with paper towels, then remove and discard the skin. Cut the fish into pieces and dust with flour.

Reserve 2–3 tablespoons of the oil and heat the remainder with the garlic cloves in a large frying pan or skillet over medium heat. When the garlic has turned golden, remove with a slotted spoon and discard. Add the pieces of salt cod to the pan and cook for 5 minutes on each side over medium heat, until evenly browned. Remove with a fish slice (spatula) and drain on paper towels.

Heat the reserved olive oil in a wide shallow pan. Add the onion and cook over low heat, stirring occasionally, for 5 minutes. Stir in the tomatoes, season with salt and pepper and cook, stirring occasionally, for 10–15 minutes.

Add the pieces of salt cod to the pan and cook for another 10 minutes. Sprinkle with the chopped parsley, if using, and serve immediately.

CECINA

Cecina

It was once customary in Livorno to ask for a 'five and five', which meant five cents' worth of bread and five cents' worth of *cecina* (chickpea cake). Older residents still have fond memories of eating 'five & five' on the streets as a mid-morning snack, when walking to school or as a quick lunch on the run. Although over the years the price has risen, the tradition of eating a 'five & five', as it is still known, is still very much alive today. A slice of *cecina* is placed between two slices of the local focaccia, sprinkled liberally with black pepper, and generally eaten while walking along: a typical Livornese street food.

Preparation time: 10 minutes
Cooking time: 20–25 minutes
Serves 4–6

- butter, for greasing
- 170 g (1½ cups) chickpea flour
- 2 tablespoons olive oil
- salt and pepper

Preheat the oven to 200°C/400°F/Gas Mark 6. Grease a large ovenproof dish with butter.

Pour 500 ml (2 cups) water into a large bowl and gradually add the chickpea flour, stirring constantly. Stir in the olive oil and a generous pinch each of salt and pepper. Pour the batter into an oven-proof sauté (frying) pan or cake tin — the batter should not be more than 1 cm (½ inch) deep. Bake for about 20–25 minutes, until the top is golden brown. Transfer to a serving plate and sprinkle with pepper. Serve hot.

TORTA RUSTICA DI NOCI E CAFFÈ

Rustic coffee and walnut cake

Walnuts are less commonly used than almonds and hazelnuts in the preparation of desserts in Tuscany. There are, however, a few specific dishes such as *torta di noci* (walnut cake) which are particularly popular across central Italy.

Preparation time: 40 minutes
Cooking time: 35–40 minutes
Serves 8–10

- 200 g (2 cups) shelled walnuts
- 120 g (½ cup) butter, softened, plus extra for greasing
- 200 g (generous 1½ cups) self-raising flour, plus extra for dusting
- 2 teaspoon baking powder
- 150 g (¾ cup) caster (superfine) sugar
- 2 large (US extra large) eggs, separated
- 100 ml (scant ½ cup) freshly brewed coffee, cooled
- ½ teaspoon vanilla extract
- salt

Preheat the oven to 180°C/350°F/Gas Mark 4. Grease and flour a ring-shaped cake pan.

Finely chop half the walnuts and coarsely chop the other half. Sift together the flour and baking powder into a bowl. Beat the butter with the sugar in another bowl. Lightly beat the egg yolks with a pinch of salt in a small bowl, then gradually beat into the butter and sugar mixture. Gradually fold in the flour mixture, alternating with the coffee, finely chopped walnuts and vanilla. Whisk the egg whites in a grease-free bowl until they form stiff peaks, then gently fold into the mixture.

Pour the mixture into the prepared cake pan and sprinkle the remaining walnuts over the cake. Put the mould on a baking sheet and bake for 50 minutes.

Remove the mould from the oven and turn out the cake onto a wire rack. Let cool completely before serving.

VIII

GROSSETO

The province of Grosseto has roots that date back to the Etruscans, traces of whom can be seen in the ancient cities of Populonia and Roselle. Much of the province's territory was for a long time considered uninhabitable, the area nearest the coast being characterized by a vast malarial expanse of marsh and salt flats. Drainage and reclamation was initiated by the Medici family and completed during the Mussolini era in the 1920s and 1930s. Nowadays a diverse and unspoiled landscape, much of which has been designated a National Park, Grosseto includes long beaches, wooded hills, volcanic rocks, natural thermal springs, green pasture, marshes and flat land.

Previous page:
The Uccellina National Park in the Maremma region of Tuscany covers an area of outstanding natural beauty, from marshlands and pine forests to sandy beaches framed by the Tyrrhenian Sea.

The province takes its culinary influences from three sources in particular: firstly, the coast; secondly, its provincial neighbour, Siena; and thirdly, a geographical area known as the Maremma, a huge tract of land to the south of the province that is divided into the Alta Maremma (upper Maremma) and the Bassa Maremma (lower Maremma). The cuisine of the area is characterized by simple ingredients of the highest quality. In the Maremma, lamb, beef and wild game feature strongly. Native to the area are the Maremmana cattle, distinguishable by their long curved horns and robust build. Used from the 1920s to the 1940s to transport marble from Monte Amiata, their numbers fell drastically with increased industrialization. But thankfully they survived and today there are around twenty thousand of these cattle, concentrated in the Maremma.

As famous as the Maremmana cattle are the *butteri*, Tuscany's answer to the cowboys of the American Wild West. Traditionally, the *butteri* controlled the movement of grazing cattle throughout the Maremma region. Although today their functions are primarily ceremonial, their skills were legendary. In fact, when Buffalo Bill brought his Wild West show to Italy in 1890, the *butteri*, unimpressed, challenged him to a contest of skills and are said to have won.

The Tuscan coastline is varied, ranging from sandy beaches to rocky shores with coves.

The range of meat dishes on offer throughout the province reflects both territory and tradition. A popular dish in the region is *Cinghiale in umido* (Wild boar stew, see page 208). Also common in the region was a dish known as *buglione* (bouillon). It was as much a method of cooking as it was a dish, a means developed by peasant families to use leftover meat often given them by their landlords. The meat would be simmered for hours until it disintegrated into a dense sauce which was then ladled over slices of bread.

The province's varied cuisine also extends to the flavours of the sea. One speciality worth mentioning is *bottarga di Orbetello* (salted mullet roe), which uses a method of preserving probably introduced by the Spanish some time in the sixteenth century. The roe is carefully extracted and pressed in salt, after which it is ready to consume after about fifteen days. There are today about sixty fishermen in Orbetello who farm mullet, and it is claimed that the best ways to eat the salted roe are either to spread it on a thick slice of Tuscan bread or serve it thinly sliced, with just a drizzle of olive oil and a squeeze of lemon juice.

Previous page:
The Maremmana cattle still graze freely in the area. Despite their long horns and impressive appearance they are in fact a very docile animal.

PASTA

Although Tuscans eat less pasta than their compatriots in other parts of Italy, the pasta dishes which can be found are both simple and delicious.

Fresh egg pasta is made throughout Tuscany. In the north, filled pasta such as *tortelli* and *ravioli* are common, a reflection of the cuisines of neighbouring Emilia-Romagna and Liguria respectively. The filling depends again on location and season, with chestnuts, cheese, potatoes, spinach, other cultivated greens, nettles and herbs taking precedence. To the south of the region, particularly in Siena, *pici* (see page 236), a rustic type of hand-made spaghetti, is popular. Also produced in the area of Siena and Grosseto are *Gnudi* (see page 202), 'nude ravioli', a type of dumpling made from ricotta and spinach, the same ingredients commonly used as the filling for ravioli or tortelli, but without the pasta casing. They are eaten all year round dressed with a simple butter and sage sauce. The classic fresh pasta of the region is pappardelle, a long, flat, ribbon pasta usually served with a duck (see page 259), hare, wild boar or mushroom sauce, depending on what is in season.

The most popular dried pasta in the region are penne (small tube-shaped pasta) which are usually served with either a vegetable or a meat sauce. Spaghetti is frequently served in restaurants along the coast with salted mullet roe, molluscs and other types of seafood.

GNUDI

Gnudi

Preparation time: 45 minutes
Cooking time: 15 minutes
Serves 4–6

- 500 g (1 lb 2 oz) spinach, coarse stalks removed
- 450 g (¾ cup) ricotta cheese
- 100 g (scant 1 cup) grated pecorino cheese, plus extra for serving
- 2 eggs, lightly beaten
- 100 g (generous ¾ cup) plain (all-purpose) flour, plus extra for dusting
- freshly grated nutmeg
- 50 g (¼ cup) butter
- 10–12 sage leaves
- salt and pepper

Put the spinach with just the water clinging to the leaves after washing into a large pan. Cook over low heat, turning once or twice, for about 3 minutes, until wilted. Drain well, squeezing out as much liquid as possible, and chop very finely. Tip into a bowl and stir in the ricotta, pecorino cheese, eggs and flour. Add the nutmeg and season with salt and pepper.

Bring a large pan of salted water to a boil. Using a teaspoon, shape small rounded dumplings from the ricotta mixture, dust with flour and add to the pan.

Cook in batches for 2–3 minutes until they float to the surface. Remove with a slotted spoon, drain on kitchen paper (paper towel) and transfer to warmed serving dish. Melt the butter with sage in another pan, then pour this over the dumplings and serve.

SUGO DI FEGATINI

Chicken liver sauce

The popularity of poultry livers in Tuscany dates back to the Renaissance and there are numerous dishes in which they are used, whether as the main ingredient or as one of a number. They are especially popular cooked as a sauce for pasta or used as a topping for crostini.

Preparation time: 25 minutes
Cooking time: 1¼ hours
Serves 6

- 2 celery stalks, chopped
- 2 carrots, chopped
- 1 onion, chopped
- 1 sprig flat-leaf parsley, chopped
- 5–6 chicken livers, trimmed and chopped
- 5 tablespoons olive oil, plus extra for drizzling
- 150 ml (⅔ cup) Vin Santo wine
- 250 g (9 oz) canned chopped tomatoes
- salt and pepper

Mix together the celery, carrots, onion, parsley and chicken livers in a bowl. Heat the oil in a pan, add the vegetable mixture, cover and cook over very low heat, stirring occasionally, for 1 hour, until browned. Pour in the wine and cook until the alcohol has evaporated.

Stir in the tomatoes, season with salt and pepper, re-cover the pan and simmer for another 10 minutes.

Remove the lid, add a drizzle of olive oil and remove the pan from the heat. This sauce is delicious on pappardelle or as a base for a risotto.

HUNTING IN MAREMMA

In Tuscany, hunting traditions run very deep. *Caccia* (hunting) is embedded in local history, customs and traditions, and although the number of registered hunters in Italy has declined in recent years there are still about 110,000 in Tuscany. The main types of game hunted throughout the region include hare, duck, pheasant, wild boar, deer and birds such as pigeons, magpies, crows, jays and doves.

Wild boar hunting is arguably the most popular and culturally important form of *caccia* in Tuscany. Hunters work in teams of at least fifteen, and often up to thirty or forty strong. Hunting for wild boar is a highly organized event, with every member of the team fulfilling a specific role — in the confusion of the hunt, there is no room for error. It is the responsibility of the *capo posta* (head positioner) to position hunters at various points on the periphery of the hunting zone. The *tracciatore* (tracker) is often the first in the field, charged with tracking the wild boar, along with the *canai* (dog handlers), whose role is to ensure that the dogs do not wander off track or get lost. In the Maremma, as in other parts of Tuscany, hunting is very much a social activity, with *feste* (feasts) held to mark the beginning and end of the season. It is said that in the past the *capo squadra* (team leader) of a hunting team was more influential and important than the town's mayor.

There are many variations on *Cinghiale in umido* (Wild boar stew, see page 208). In some areas the meat is marinated overnight in milk, in other areas in wine or vinegar. In all cases, however, the meat is cooked slowly until it is deliciously tender.

Hunting in Maremma is hugely popular. Hunters are almost always accompanied by hunting dogs.

CINGHIALE IN UMIDO

Wild boar stew

In Tuscany, when a group of huntsmen is lucky enough to bag several animals, the division of the meat among the participants also includes the 'dogs' share', an identical quantity to that of their owners.

Preparation time: 25 minutes + overnight marinating
Cooking time: 3 hours
Serves 6

- 1 litre (4 ¼ cups) white wine vinegar
- 1 × 2-kg (4 ½-lb) leg of wild boar, boned
- 5 tablespoons olive oil
- 1 clove garlic, peeled
- 1 sprig rosemary
- 2 celery stalks, finely chopped
- 2 carrots, finely chopped
- 1 onion, finely chopped
- 200 g (1 ¾ cups) minced (ground) beef
- 250 g (9 oz) canned chopped tomatoes
- 1 tablespoon tomato purée (paste)
- pinch of chilli powder
- 2 bay leaves
- pinch of crushed pink peppercorns
- salt
- polenta or puréed potatoes, to serve

Pour the vinegar into a shallow dish, add the meat, turning to coat, cover and let marinate in the refrigerator overnight.

Drain the meat well, discarding the marinade. Cut it into 2.5-cm (1-inch) cubes. Heat 3 tablespoons of the oil in a shallow pan with the garlic clove and rosemary sprig. When the garlic has turned golden brown, remove it and the rosemary with a slotted spoon and discard. Add the cubes of meat and cook over medium-high heat, stirring frequently, for 5–8 minutes, until evenly browned. Remove the pan from the heat.

Heat the remaining oil in another shallow pan. Add the celery, carrots and onion and cook over low heat, stirring occasionally, for 5 minutes, until softened. Add the minced (ground) beef, increase the heat to medium and cook, stirring frequently and breaking it up with the spoon, for 5–8 minutes, until evenly browned. Stir in the cubes of meat, then stir in the tomatoes, tomato purée (paste), chilli powder and bay leaves and season with salt and crushed pink peppercorns. Reduce the heat, cover and simmer gently for 2½ hours, until the meat is very tender.

Transfer the stew to a warmed serving dish and serve immediately with polenta or puréed potatoes.

FAGIANO IN SALMI ALLA TOSCANA

Tuscan-style pheasant salmis

Tuscan-style pheasant salmis, a dish of Franco-Piedmontese origin, is known also as *civet*. Adopted, with a few changes, by the Tuscan middle classes in the early twentieth century, the dish has been popular in the region ever since.

Preparation time: 20 minutes + 3–4 hours for marinating
Cooking time: 50 minutes
Serves 6

- 1 carrot, chopped
- 1 celery stalk, chopped
- 1 onion, chopped
- 2–3 sage leaves, chopped
- 1 sprig rosemary, chopped
- 2 cloves garlic, chopped
- grated zest of 1 lemon
- juice of ½ lemon, strained
- 3–4 tablespoons olive oil
- 6 pheasant breasts
- 175 ml (¾ cup) dry white wine
- 175 ml (¾ cup) chicken stock
- salt and pepper

Mix together the carrot, celery, onion, sage, rosemary, garlic, lemon zest and juice and the oil in a large, shallow dish and season with salt and pepper. Add the pheasant breasts, turning to coat, cover and let marinate for 3–4 hours.

Transfer the pheasant and all the marinade to a flameproof casserole and cook over medium heat, stirring occasionally, for 15 minutes. Pour in the wine and cook for a few minutes until the alcohol has evaporated. Pour in the stock and bring to a boil, then reduce the heat, cover and simmer for 30 minutes. Remove the casserole from the heat and serve immediately.

CONIGLIO IN PORCHETTA

Rabbit in porchetta

'*In porchetta*' ('pork style') is a method for seasoning meat. It takes its name from the *porchetta*, a dish which involves a whole pig being boned, stuffed with a mix of herbs and spices including, most importantly, wild fennel, then trussed and roasted; sometimes on a spit over an open fire. The same method is used today to cook a range of meat including rabbit, goose, duck and chicken.

Preparation time: 30 minutes + 1 hour for marinating
Cooking time: 1 hour 40 minutes
Serves 6

- 1 × 2.25-kg (5-lb) skinned and cleaned rabbit, boned, liver reserved
- 200 ml (scant 1 cup) white wine vinegar
- 3 sprigs sage, chopped
- 3 sprigs rosemary, chopped
- 3 sprigs wild fennel, chopped
- 1 clove garlic, chopped
- 200 g (7 oz) prosciutto, sliced
- 25g (2 tablespoons) butter
- 3 tablespoons olive oil
- 100 ml (scant ½ cup) dry white wine
- 1 bay leaf
- pepper

Put the rabbit into a shallow dish. Mix together the vinegar and 400 ml (1¾ cups) water, pour the mixture into the dish and let marinate for 1 hour.

Remove the rabbit from the dish, rinse under cold running water and pat dry with paper towels.

Trim and chop the liver, then mix with the sage, rosemary, fennel and garlic. Open out the rabbit and spread half the herb mixture in the cavity. Season generously with pepper, put the slices of prosciutto on top and sprinkle with the remaining herb mixture.

Roll up the rabbit as tightly as possible and tie with trussing thread or kitchen string. Melt the butter with the oil in a large oval pan. Add the rabbit and cook over medium-high heat, turning frequently, for 10 minutes, until evenly browned. Pour in the wine and cook for a few minutes until the alcohol has evaporated. Add the bay leaf, reduce the heat, cover and simmer, adding a little hot water if necessary, for 1½ hours, until tender and cooked through. Remove the pan from the heat and let cool completely. Lift out the rabbit, remove and discard the string and cut into slices to serve.

SFORMATO DI GOBBI

Cardoon mould

Preparation time: 30 minutes
Cooking time: 2 hours 30 minutes
Serves 6

- juice of 1 lemon
- 500 g (1 lb 2 oz) cardoons
- 25 g (2 tablespoons) butter, plus extra for greasing
- 175 ml (¾ cup) milk
- 4 eggs
- 50 g (⅔ cup) grated Parmesan cheese
- salt

For the béchamel sauce:

- 25 g (2 tablespoons) butter
- 2 tablespoons plain (all-purpose) flour
- 250 ml (1 cup) milk
- pinch of freshly grated nutmeg
- salt and pepper

Pour plenty of water into a large pan and add the lemon juice and a pinch of salt. Trim the cardoons, cut the inner stalks into 5-cm (2-inch) lengths and remove all strings, immediately dropping the pieces into the acidulated water to prevent discolouration. Bring to a boil, then reduce the heat and simmer 35–40 minutes.

Drain the cardoons. Melt the butter in a shallow pan. Add the cardoons and cook over medium-low heat for a few minutes. Reduce the heat, pour in the milk and simmer for 30 minutes.

Meanwhile, make the béchamel sauce. Melt the butter in a pan over medium heat. Whisk in the flour. Pour in all the milk, whisking constantly until it comes to a boil. Reduce the heat and simmer gently, stirring occasionally, for 20 minutes. Remove the pan from the heat, stir in the nutmeg and taste and adjust the seasoning, if necessary. Preheat the oven to 160°C/325°F/Gas Mark 3. Grease an ovenproof mould with butter. Transfer the cardoons to a food processor or blender and process to a purée or chop them finely.

Add the purée to the béchamel sauce and stir in the eggs and Parmesan. Season to taste with salt and mix thoroughly. Pour the mixture into the prepared mould and put the mould into a roasting pan. Pour in hot water to come about halfway up the side and bake for 35–40 minutes until set. Remove the mould from the oven and let stand for 5 minutes, then turn out onto a warmed serving dish and serve immediately.

TORTINO DI FIORI DI ZUCCA RIPIENI

Stuffed courgette (zucchini) flower tart

Courgette (zucchini) flowers are popular throughout Tuscany and central Italy. They can be stuffed, sautéed or used as a filling for an omelette. In the absence of courgette flowers, pumpkin flowers are an excellent alternative.

Preparation time: 30 minutes
Cooking time: 45 minutes including 5 minutes for resting
Serves 4

- 100 g (scant 1 cup) minced (ground) beef
- 100 g Tuscan sausage, skinned
- 1 clove garlic, chopped
- 4–5 tarragon leaves, chopped
- 6 eggs
- 50 g (⅔ cup) grated Parmesan cheese
- 1–2 tablespoons breadcrumbs (optional)
- 12 large courgette (zucchini) flowers, pistils removed
- butter, for greasing
- 2 tablespoons olive oil
- 1 small onion, finely chopped
- 2 tablespoons tomato sauce
- salt and pepper

Mix together the beef, sausage meat, garlic, tarragon and 1 egg in a bowl. Reserve 2 tablespoons of the Parmesan and add the remainder to the bowl. Season lightly with salt and pepper. Work the mixture with a wooden spoon until it becomes smooth, gradually adding the breadcrumbs if necessary. Stuff the courgette (zucchini) flowers with the mixture.

Preheat the oven to 180°C/350°F/Gas Mark 4 and grease a round 20-cm (8-inch) cake pan with butter.

Heat the oil in a pan. Add the onion and cook over low heat, stirring occasionally, for 5 minutes. Carefully add the stuffed flowers and cook until golden brown and the stuffing mixture is cooked through. Remove the pan from the heat and transfer the flowers to the prepared pan.

Beat the remaining eggs with the remaining Parmesan and the tomato sauce in a bowl, season with salt and pepper and pour the mixture into the pan. Put the pan on a baking sheet and bake for 20 minutes until mixture is first to the touch. Remove the pan from the oven and let stand for 5 minutes, then turn out and serve immediately.

IX

SIENA

The Torre del Mangia (Tower of the Eater), Siena's distinctive belltower, was built between 1325 and 1344 and is named after its first guardian, Giovanni di Duccio, nicknamed *mangiaguadagni* ('eat your earnings') for his tendency to spend all his money on food. Every year the bells of the Torre del Mangia ring to signal the final procession which precedes the *Palio*, the famous horse race that pits the seventeen *contrade* (districts) of the city against each other. Loyalty to a *contrada* runs deep; it is an allegiance that is inherited at birth and endures for a lifetime. The spectacle, with the participants in full medieval costume, is a fiery and passionate event which has come to symbolize the city and people of Siena to the world.

Previous page:
A typical Chianti cellar, where wines must be aged in oak barrels for a minimum of seven months before bottling in order to qualify as DOCG (which is an Italian quality assurance label).

The landscape of the province of Siena is quintessentially Tuscan, a picture postcard image of rolling hills, vineyards and olive groves. Medieval towns, seemingly trapped in a time warp, stand majestically on hilltops, a living testimony to the past. One of the most beautiful is San Gimignano, its distinctive towers — only fifteen of the original seventy-two remain standing — a treasured architectural feature of the Tuscan skyline. It was the saffron trade that enabled the city's wealthiest inhabitants to build the towers, and the size of one's tower was, at the time, considered a status symbol. Saffron has been cultivated in the area since at least the Middle Ages. In 1228 the Town Council paid the debts it had incurred during a military siege partly in saffron. By 1295, so great was the export value of saffron that the Council assigned two special keepers to the city gates, charged with levying export duty.

The area's saffron is still renowned for its quality. No artificial chemicals are used at any stage of its cultivation, and the saffron stamens are packaged whole in order to ensure their purity and to protect their pungent, slightly bitter aroma. Today, saffron fields harmoniously coexist alongside ancient olive groves and vines. Siena's countryside is best represented in Ambrogio Lorenzetti's painting *Good Government*,

The town of San Gimignano rises above the hills dominating the Elsa Valley. After his visit, E.M. Forster used the town as the inspiration for his 1905 novel *Where Angels Fear to Tread*.

which hangs in the city's Civic Museum: it depicts the famed Cinta Senese pig set against a background of perfectly ordered and well-managed farmland.

Previous page:
At 102 metres (335 feet) tall, the Torre del Mangia located in Siena's shell-shaped Piazza del Campo, is visible from all districts of the city.

Siena's cuisine is straightforward and unpretentious, focusing on flavours that are intense yet simple. Such was the renown of the region's cuisine that in the sixteenth century Catherine de' Medici selected a number of Sienese cooks to accompany her to the French court when she married King Henri II. Particularly noteworthy is the pecorino di Pienza, a highly regarded pecorino produced in an area known as the Crete Sinesi. A favourite cheese of Lorenzo the Magnificent, the famous fifteenth-century head of the powerful Medici family, pecorino di Pienza is made with milk from the Sarda breed of sheep which graze on the pastures of the region. The cheeses, often wrapped in walnut leaves, are left to mature in humid cellars. Alternatively the cheeses can be matured for up to ninety days in barrels formerly used to age great wines such as Brunello di Montalcino. The latter cheese is known as *pecorino di Pienza stagionato in barrique*. Mature pecorino, which is aged for up to eighteen months, is especially suited to grating over pasta, whilst the fresher cheeses pair superbly with chestnut honey from Montalcino and any of the local wines.

Indeed, when it comes to wine, few would disagree that the province of Siena is home to some of the best in the world. In addition to Chianti Classico and the white Vernaccia wines of San Gimignano, since 1888 the area has been home to the esteemed Brunello di Montalcino, a red wine made entirely with the Sangiovese Gross grape variety and aged for four years before being sold.

THE CINTA SENESE PIG

The Cinta Senese, Tuscany's distinctive breed of pig, goes back at least to the medieval period. Representations of it can be seen in paintings and frescoes dating from the twelth century in churches throughout Tuscany.

The breed takes its name from the characteristic white belt (*cinta*) on its dark grey or black coat. The Cinta Senese is a rustic pig, semi-wild and happy to forage on a diet of acorns, chestnuts and apples, supplemented with other locally grown organic food. Once widespread throughout the Tuscan countryside, from the 1960s their numbers fell drastically following the importation of other breeds from elsewhere in Europe. But since the turn of the century, growing appreciation of top-quality meat has led to a reversal of this trend and the Cinta Senese is making a comeback. Today, a full range of traditional *salume* (cured meat) products is produced from the Cinta Senese, and demand often outstrips supply.

SAUSAGES AND MEAT PRODUCTS

Salume is the generic name in Italian for all salted and cured meat products. They generally fall into two broad categories. The first are called *insaccati* (literally 'in a casing'). This group includes the common cylindrical salami, the one most frequently encountered in Tuscany being the *finocchiona toscana*. Like good wine, salami mirrors the tastes and flavours of the land from which it comes. The *finocchiona* is no exception, its intense aroma and distinctive flavour owed in large part to a seasoning of local garlic, red wine and wild fennel, from which it derives its name.

Following page:
The Cinta Senese pig, an ancient breed, is the only pig native to Tuscany that has survived extinction.

The second group includes *salume* made from a whole piece of meat, such as *prosciutto* (cured ham), *lardo* (cured back fat) and *pancetta* (cured pork belly or side). The most familiar of these is the *prosciutto di Toscana,* a ham produced throughout the region, which has PDO or protected origin, status. The meat is salted, cured in a mix of local herbs and spices, and aged for a year, resulting in a ham that is bright to light red in colour and full of flavour. It is considered the perfect accompaniment to the local unsalted bread.

Founded in 1729, the Antica Macelleria Falorni in Greve, in Chianti, continues to sell traditional Tuscan cured meat products from locally sourced meats, such as wild boar and the Cinta Senese pig.

Other *salumi* produced throughout the region include a wide range of artisan products made on a small scale. Worth looking out for are the various *salumi* made from the Cinta Senese pig, as well as *salame di cinghiale* (wild boar salami), a fennel-flavoured *pancetta* from Pisa called *rigatino finocchiato*, and *bazzone* ham from the Garfagnana region in Lucca. The last of these takes its name from the shape of the ham, which is said to resemble a pronounced chin (*bazzo* or *bazza* in the local dialect), and is made from the meat of semi-wild pigs that forage in the mountainous landscape. Finally, *buristo toscano* is a black pudding (blood sausage) made in various forms all over the region. A particularly good one is the *buristo senese*, made in the Chianti region of Siena between November and March. The sausage, which is flavoured with lemon zest, parsley, garlic, pine nuts and sultanas, should be eaten fresh — sliced and sautéed, with a splash of wine in the pan to finish.

RAVIGGIOLO

Raviggiolo

Usually made with sheep's milk in Tuscany, *raviggiolo* is a soft, fresh cheese with a very delicate flavour. The name comes from the town of Raggiolo in the Pratomagno region, a mountainous area near Florence. The most prized *raviggiolo* is that from Sarteano in Siena. It is also very pleasant when served with a red fruit jam on the side.

Preparation time: 10 minutes + 3 hours standing
Cooking time: 35 minutes
Serves 4–6

- 1 litre (4 ¼ cups) full-fat (whole) milk
- 1 ½ tablespoons liquid rennet, or 1 ½ tablets rennet dissolved in 50 ml (¼ cup) water
- 1 teaspoon salt
- 2 tablespoons vinegar
- pesto sauce or basil-flavoured olive oil, to serve

Warm a large pan of water to 40°C/110°F. Meanwhile, pour the milk into another pan, place it over low heat and stir gently until the temperature reaches 38–40°C/100–104°F. Add the rennet, salt and vinegar, and stir for a few seconds more. Cover the pan and transfer it to the large pan of hot water. This acts as a bain-marie to keep the temperature constant (the water in the bain-marie must be a degree or so higher than the temperature of the milk). Let stand for 1 hour, until curd forms and the whey (watery liquid) separates.

Line a sieve with a double layer of muslin that has been sterilized with boiling water. Place over a bowl. Spoon the curd into the sieve and allow to drain for at least two hours.

Transfer it to a terrine using a slotted spoon and serve as an antipasto, flavoured with a little pesto sauce or with a few drops of basil-flavoured oil.

The cheese will keep for about two days in the refridgerator.

RIBOLLITA

Although this dish has achieved iconic status in recent years, and is served today in restaurants throughout Tuscany, it is important to remember that it is the humble offspring of peasant cookery. The name *ribollita* (literally 'reboiled', see page 234) refers to the method of cooking: it is, in effect, a reheated version of leftover vegetables or beans as a soup, served sometimes with sliced onions but always with olive oil and freshly ground black pepper. The practice may have originated as a means of using up stewed beans left over from Friday, traditionally considered a lean day when the Church prohibited the consumption of meat.

Both methods of cooking and ingredients vary widely. Beans of some variety, cavolo nero and toasted stale bread are, however, essential. A dense texture is required in the finished soup, and this is usually achieved by puréeing some or all of the beans. In one version, alternate layers of toasted bread, beans and cooked vegetables are moistened with a vegetable broth, after which the whole dish is heated in the oven until a crust forms on top. The second cooking takes full advantage of the enhanced flavours that vegetables acquire when reheated, and of the intensified aromas of toasted bread. *Ribollita* is always finished with a healthy drizzle of Tuscan extra-virgin olive oil.

Pulses (legumes), such as the creamy white cannellini bean, are often sold by the *etto* (100 g/3½oz) in their dried form and are enjoyed eaten on their own or added to soups or stews.

RIBOLLITA

Ribollita

In some areas of Tuscany, ham fat and bacon rind are also added to the vegetables.

Preparation time: 30 minutes
Cooking time: 2 hours 40 minutes
Serves 4–6

- 500 g (2 ¾ cups) dried cannellini beans, soaked overnight in water to cover and drained
- 3 tablespoons olive oil
- 1 onion, chopped
- 1 celery stalk, chopped
- 2–3 carrots, chopped
- 2 potatoes, diced
- 1–2 courgettes (zucchini), sliced
- 1 bunch Swiss chard leaves, shredded
- 1 Savoy or summer cabbage, or a bunch of cavolo nero, shredded
- 1 sprig flat-leaf parsley, chopped
- day-old rustic loaf, very thinly sliced
- salt and pepper

Put the cannellini beans into a large pan, pour in water to cover and bring to a boil. Reduce the heat and simmer for 40 minutes.

Meanwhile, heat the oil in another large pan. Add the onion, celery, carrots, potatoes and courgettes (zucchini) and cook over very low heat, stirring occasionally, for 30 minutes. Season with salt, add the Swiss chard and cabbage and cook, stirring, for a few minutes. Cover the pan.

Drain the beans, reserving the cooking liquid. Press half the beans through a sieve (sifter) into a bowl, then stir the purée into the pan of vegetables. Add the reserved cooking liquid and simmer for 1 hour. Add the remaining whole beans and parsley and simmer for another 1–1½ hours.

Remove the soup from the heat and season with salt and pepper to taste. Make a layer of bread slices in a tureen and ladle some of the soup over it. Continue making alternate layers of bread and soup until all the ingredients have been used, then let stand until the bread is completely soaked. Serve immediately.

PICI

Pici are a coarse type of *spaghettoni* (large spaghetti) which are claimed to have originated in southern Tuscany and are especially popular in the province of Siena. Traditionally made by hand using only flour, water and a pinch of salt (the addition of egg being more recent), they have a coarse texture and irregular shape which make them perfect for holding a sauce. *Pici all'Etrusca* (with a sauce of hard-boiled eggs, garlic and herbs, see page 238) was a popular peasant dish. On more affluent tables the pasta was topped with rich meat-based sauces, and in mountainous regions with mushrooms. In Celle sul Rigo, a small medieval town just outside Siena, a festival called the *Sagra dei pici* (Pici festival) is held every May to celebrate this distinctive Tuscan speciality.

Egg pasta such as *pappardelle* or *tagliatelle* usually reign supreme in Tuscany with one notable exception — *pici*, the famous local pasta of Siena, traditionally made without eggs.

La Novella
Pasta di Semola di Grano Duro
Trafilata al bronzo - Essicazione Lenta
Pici
COTTUra 22 MINUTI
500 g

PICI ALL'ETRUSCA

Etruscan-style pici

The name comes from the Italian verb *appiccicare* (to stick together). The pasta dough is rolled out to 2 cm (¾ inch) thick and then cut into small diamond shapes. With the fingertips outstretched, these are rolled backwards and forwards by hand to make them long and thin like spaghetti. Dried pici can also be found in Italian speciality shops.

Preparation time: 1 hour + 30 minutes for resting
Cooking time: 5 minutes
Serves 4

For the pasta:

- 200 g (1 ¾ cups) plain (all-purpose) flour, preferably Italian type 00
- 200 g (generous 1 cup) semolina
- salt

For the sauce:

- 1 hard-boiled egg
- 5–6 cloves garlic
- 1 sprig flat-leaf parsley
- 6 basil leaves
- 6 mint leaves
- 120–150 ml (½–⅔ cup) olive oil
- grated pecorino cheese, for sprinkling
- salt and pepper

To make the pici, mix together the flour, semolina and a pinch of salt in a bowl. Gradually mix in enough water to make a firm, elastic dough. Shape the dough into a ball, wrap in a clean dish towel and let rest for 30 minutes.

Meanwhile, make the sauce. Chop the hard-boiled egg with the garlic, parsley, basil and mint, then transfer the mixture to a bowl. Gradually drizzle in enough oil to make a fairly liquid sauce. Season to taste with salt and pepper.

Unwrap the pasta. Taking a small piece at a time, rub it back and forth on the work surface (counter) with your fingertips until it resembles thick spaghetti. Bring a large pan of salted water to a boil. Add the pasta, bring back to a boil and cook for 2–3 minutes, until tender but still firm to the bite. Drain, add to the sauce and toss well. Transfer to a serving dish, sprinkle with grated pecorino and serve immediately.

CAPPONE CON I GOBBI

Capon with cardoons

Preparation time: 1½ hours
Cooking time: 2½ hours
Serves 8

- 1 × 3-kg (6¾-lb) capon (or chicken or guinea fowl), liver reserved
- juice of 1 lemon, strained
- 1 kg (2¼ lb) cardoons
- 200 g (1¾ cups) plain (all-purpose) flour
- 1 egg
- 250 ml (scant 1 cup) milk
- 500 g (1 lb 2 oz) minced (ground) pork
- 2 onions, thinly sliced
- 1 sprig flat-leaf parsley, chopped
- 150 ml (⅔ cup) olive oil
- 6 ripe tomatoes, peeled, seeded and chopped
- vegetable oil, for deep-frying
- salt

Trim and chop the liver, then set aside. Cut the bird into 10 pieces, put into a large pan and pour in water to cover. Add a large pinch of salt and bring to a boil. Reduce the heat and simmer for 1½–2 hours, until tender. Remove the pieces with tongs. Meanwhile, fill a large pan with water and stir in the lemon juice. Remove and discard the tough outer stalks from the cardoons. Trim off the tips from the remaining stalks and cut them into 5–7.5-cm (2–3-inch) pieces, immediately adding them to the acidulated water to prevent discolouration. Add a pinch of salt to the pan and bring to the boil. Reduce the heat and simmer for 45–60 minutes, until tender. Drain and set aside.

While they are cooking, prepare a batter. Sift the flour with a pinch of salt into a bowl and make a well in the centre. Add the egg to the well and beat with a whisk or wooden spoon. Gradually whisk in the milk, a little at a time, until smooth. If the batter is too thick, whisk in 3–4 tablespoons water. Cover and let rest. Put the pork, onions, parsley and olive oil into a large pan. Stir in the tomatoes, capon liver and pieces of capon. Season with salt. Cook over low heat for 25–28 minutes, stir occasionally and add a little water if necessary.

Stir the cardoons into the batter. Heat the vegetable oil in a deep-fryer to 180–190°C/350–375°F or until a cube of day-old bread browns in 30 seconds. Using tongs, add the cardoons to the hot oil, a few pieces at a time, and cook until crisp and golden brown. Remove with a slotted spoon and drain on paper towels. Remove the pieces of capon from the pan and put them on a serving dish. Add the cardoons to the pan and simmer for 5 minutes. Spoon the cardoons and sauce over the meat and serve immediately.

THE PANFORTE OF SIENA

Panforte (see page 244), a delicious, dense sweetmeat, has long been associated with the city of Siena and the tradition of the Palio, the famous horse race that takes place in its streets. It has been claimed that the seventeen basic ingredients specified in one of the earliest mentioned recipes refer to the seventeen *contrade* (districts) of the city. Although the exact origin remains unclear, *panforte* most probably originated in the thirteenth century as a variation on *panpepato* (a rich chocolate dessert) and *pan melato* (a fruit bread enriched with honey).

There are two types of *panforte*. The darker, more traditional recipe uses almonds, roasted walnuts, and candied orange and melon peel along with a mix of spices including cinnamon and coriander. The light version, invented in 1879 and named *Panforte Margherita* in honour of Queen Margherita of Savoy, substitutes lemon for the melon peel and adds a final dusting of icing sugar. Another well-known variation is the chocolate *panforte* created in 1820 by a pastry chef named Giovanni Parenti, and known as *Panforte delle dame* (ladies' *panforte*) because of its more delicate taste.

The imposing Palazzo Pubblico (town hall) is located in the centre of the city's main square, Piazza del Campo. Built in the thirteenth century, Siena's city council still governs from here.

PANFORTE DI SIENA

Panforte from Siena

Preparation time: 30 minutes
Cooking time: 30 minutes
Serves 4–6

- butter for greasing
- 150 g (⅔ cup) clear honey
- 200 g (1 ¾ cup) icing (confectioners') sugar plus extra for dusting
- 160 g (1 ⅔ cup) plain flour
- 300 g whole blanched almonds
- 200 g candied peel
- Grated zest of 3 untreated oranges
- ½ teaspoon ground cinnamon, plus extra for dusting (optional)
- ¼ teaspoon ground nutmeg
- ¼ teaspoon allspice
- pinch of ground black pepper
- a few sheets of rice paper

Preheat the oven to 150°C/300°F/Gas Mark 2. Line the base of a 24-cm (9½-inch) springform baking tin with the rice paper and grease and line the sides with baking parchment.

Place the honey and icing sugar in a large heavy-based pan and melt together over a medium heat taking care not to let it burn. In a separate bowl mix together the flour, almonds, candied peel, orange zest and spices.

When the honey mixture begins to bubble around the edge add the flour mixture and 70 ml (generous ¼ cup) of water. Stir everything together well and continue stirring over the heat for a few minutes until the mixture begins to get a little sticky. Pour the mixture into the prepared baking tin and bake in the preheated oven for 30 minutes. Allow to cool completely and then dust generously with icing sugar, adding a ½ teaspoon of cinnamon to the icing sugar if desired.

X

AREZZO

FERROVIA
AREZZO -
CITTÀ DI CASTELLO
FOSSATO
ORARIO a datare dal 1° Novembre 1905.
STAZIONI
ANGHIARI
AREZZO
GUBBIO
CITTÀ DI CASTELLO

Previous page:
Olives destined for olive oil production must be harvested just before their peak of ripeness. Too soon and the oil will be bitter, too late and it will lose all pungency.

The province of Arezzo is dominated by three large valleys: the Casentino, the Val di Chiana and the Valdarno. The Arno, Tuscany's longest river, rises on Mount Falterona in the north of the province, flowing down through the Casentino National Park towards the central plain of Arezzo where it curves westwards towards Florence.

Inhabited since Etruscan times, the landscape of Arezzo remains largely unchanged, characterized by centuries-old forests, picturesque hilltop villages and towns, feudal castles, Romanesque churches and ancient Roman ruins. The valleys are dotted with family-run vineyards, orchards and olive groves.

The cuisine of Arezzo is unpretentious, wholesome and tasty. A note of self-sufficiency is evident in the province, with smallholdings producing much of a family's requirements. Farmyard fowl such as chickens, duck, guinea fowl and geese have had a particularly high value in the area, constituting the mainstay of the diet. Many farms in the area breed the *pollo del Valdarno* or *Valdarnese Bianca*, an ancient Tuscan breed of poultry.

In Arezzo, as in every part of Tuscany, locally produced olive oil and unsalted bread still constitute both the starting and finishing touch for many local dishes. The twin love affairs with poultry and bread are perfectly harmonized in the popular antipasto called *Crostini neri all' aretina* (Aretina-style black crostini, see page 256), a flavourful mix of chicken livers, spleen, onions, anchovies, capers and parsley cooked in white wine and spooned onto toasted bread.

Poultry is also the basis of the area's most popular pasta dish, *Pappardelle con anatra* (Pappardelle with duck, see page 259). It was once called *pappardelle sulla nana* — *nana* being an old and affectionate word for 'duck' in Arezzo. Over the course of the hunting season, the dish is often made with hare, rabbit or other game.

Rabbit, both wild and farmed, remains one of the most commonly used meats in Arezzo and features in dishes such *Coniglio arrosto all'aretina* (Aretina-style roast rabbit, see page 260). Wild rabbits, which are smaller in size than hare, are always popular during the hunting season. However, farmed rabbits have been bred in the region as far back as the medieval period, both as a source of food and for their hides.

Up until a few decades ago, rabbits were only bred at the family level or on small holdings as a means of accruing a little additional income. However, today they are bred on a much larger scale to the extent that Italy has attained first place globally both for production and consumption.

Today, rabbit can be bought in many ways — either whole or just the saddle which is considered ideal for roasting. Alternatively the back quarters can be bought whole which can be deboned, stuffed and rolled or cut into pieces for a stew. Rabbit is a white meat and if it is fed and cooked properly, the meat should be tender with a wonderfully intense flavour.

CHIANINA CATTLE

In terms of size, the white Chianina ox is the largest breed of cattle in the world. They have ancient origins: large white cattle, most likely the Chianina, were known as early as Roman times. The Romans revered them for their beauty and strength rather than for gastronomic reasons, and they were often brought to Rome to take part in sacrificial processions.

A fixture of the Tuscan landscape, the Chianina originated in western central Italy, and the largest of them are to be found in the Val di Chiana in the provinces of Arezzo and Siena. Traditionally they were used as a draught animal, their exceptional strength and docile disposition making them indispensable on farms. With the advent of mechanized farming, emphasis shifted to their potential for producing beef. In this regard they are highly esteemed. The *Bistecca alla fiorentina* (Florentine-style steak, see page 138), unquestionably one of Tuscany's signature dishes, is traditionally prepared from Chianina beef.

Following page:
The porcelain-white Chianina cow is renowned for its remarkably tender, marbled meat. A true *bistecca alla fiorentina* (see page 138) should be made with this beef only.

TUSCAN BREAD

In Tuscany, more than any other region in Italy, bread is the foundation of every meal, surpassing even pasta and rice as the main staple. It is one of the essential ingredients of the kitchen, used not just as an accompaniment, but also as an integral component in many dishes.

First-time visitors to the Tuscan table usually remark on the fact that the bread is made without salt. One theory has it that the tradition dates back to the twelfth century when Pisa, where the salt came from, levied unduly heavy import taxes on their saltless rivals, Florence. Rather than pay the exorbitant price, Florentine bakers learned to do without.

Yet, although the bread contains no salt, it is no less flavoursome and, as visitors quickly discover, it is in fact the perfect accompaniment to the rest of Tuscan food, which is in itself tasty and full of flavour. The local *prosciutto*, *salami* and other cured meats, which are well seasoned, seem deliberately designed to match the bread, as do the hearty soups and rich stews.

Often in cooking, Tuscans will use bread that is at least a day old. It is a practice that dates back to a time when poverty dictated that nothing could ever be wasted. *Pane raffermo*, as it is known, deserves none of the negative connotations of its literal translation, 'stale bread'. A more fitting description would be 'mature and firm'. The repertoire of recipes in which stale bread is put to use includes many of the more widely recognized Tuscan dishes. It is used to start the meal with *fett' unta* (stale bread rubbed with garlic and drizzled with olive oil) or with the more elaborate *crostini*. It is also used in soups like *Ribollita* (see page 234) and *Pappa col pomodoro* (Tomato and bread soup, see page 130), and as a base to soak up the juices of both meat and fish stews such as *Cacciucco alla livornese* (Livornese-style cacciucco, see page 182).

Tuscan bread is put to many uses in the kitchen. At its simplest, it is toasted, rubbed with garlic, a drizzle of olive oil and a sprinkle of fresh herbs.

CROSTINI NERI ALL'ARETINA

Aretina-style black crostini

The words *crostini*, *crostoni* and *bruschetta* are used interchangeably to describe a slice of bread with a topping. However, smaller bite-sized pieces of bread are generally referred to as *crostini*. In Tuscany toppings can be as simple as a rub of garlic and a drizzle of olive oil to more elaborate toppings such as the recipe described below.

Preparation time: 15 minutes
Cooking time: 20–25 minutes
Serves 8

- 50 g (¼ cup) butter
- 3 tablespoons olive oil
- 1 white onion, thinly sliced
- 2 tablespoons chopped flat-leaf parsley
- 300 g (11 oz) chicken livers, trimmed
- 5 tablespoons dry Vin Santo or other white wine
- 175 ml (¾ cup) beef stock
- 250 g (9 oz) calf's spleen or liver, chopped
- 1–2 canned anchovies, drained and chopped
- 1 tablespoon chopped capers
- salt and pepper
- thin slices Tuscan bread, toasted, to serve

Melt half the butter with the oil in a frying pan or skillet. Add the onion, parsley and chicken livers and cook for a few minutes over medium-high heat, stirring frequently, for 5 minutes. Reduce the heat to medium-low and cook, stirring frequently, for another 10 minutes. Pour in the wine and cook for a few minutes until the alcohol has evaporated, then season with pepper and remove the pan from the heat.

Turn out the mixture on to a chopping (cutting) board and chop with a mezzaluna or a heavy kitchen knife Transfer the mixture to a shallow pan and add the remaining butter, the stock and the chopped calf's spleen or liver.

Cook over low heat, stirring occasionally, for a few minutes, but do not let the mixture dry out. Remove the pan from the heat, add the anchovies and capers, season lightly with salt and mix well. Briefly dip 1 side of each slice of toast in the hot stock and spoon some of the liver mixture on top. Arrange on a serving dish and serve immediately.

PAPPARDELLE CON ANATRA

Preparation time: 1 hour
Cooking time: 55 minutes
Serves 4

Pappardelle with duck

- 2 tablespoons olive oil
- 1 x 1.75-kg (4-lb) cleaned, skinned and deboned duck, cut into bite-sized pieces
- 1 carrot, finely chopped
- 1 onion, finely chopped
- 1 celery stalk, finely chopped
- 1 sprig flat-leaf parsley, finely chopped
- 1 sprig thyme, finely chopped
- 1 sprig marjoram, finely chopped
- 1 duck liver, trimmed and chopped, or 150 g (¼ cup) minced (ground) pork
- 175 ml (¾ cup) dry white wine
- 1 tablespoon tomato purée (paste) or 2–3 tomatoes, peeled, seeded and chopped
- salt and pepper
- grated Parmesan cheese, for sprinkling

For the pappardelle:

- 200 g (1¾ cups) plain (all-purpose) flour, preferably Italian type 00, plus extra for dusting
- 2 eggs
- salt

Heat the oil in a large pan. Add the pieces of duck and cook over medium high heat, turning frequently, for 5 minutes. Season with salt and pepper, reduce the heat to low, cover and cook, turning occasionally, for 5–10 minutes, until well browned. Remove the meat from the pan with a slotted spoon and set aside.

Add the carrot, onion, celery, parsley, thyme and marjoram to the pan and cook over low heat, stirring occasionally, for 3 minutes. Add the liver or minced (ground) meat, season with salt and pepper and cook, stirring frequently, for 10 minutes, until evenly browned. Return the duck to the pan, pour in the wine and cook until the alcohol has evaporated. Mix the tomato purée (paste), if using, with 2 tablespoons hot water in a small bowl and stir it into the pan or stir in the tomatoes. Simmer for 30 minutes.

To make the pappardelle, sift the flour with a pinch of salt into a mound on a work surface (counter) and make a well in the centre. Break the eggs into the well and, using your fingers, gradually incorporate the flour, then knead for about 10 minutes, until smooth and elastic. Roll out the dough on a lightly floured surface and let dry for 10 minutes. Using a pasta cutting wheel or sharp knife, cut out ribbons 20 cm (8 inches) long and 3 cm (1¼ inches) wide, then cut them in half.

Bring a large pan of salted water to a boil. Add the pappardelle, bring back to a boil and cook for 3–4 minutes, until tender but still firm to the bite. Drain and tip into a warmed serving dish. Spoon the sauce on top, sprinkle with Parmesan and serve immediately.

CONIGLIO ARROSTO ALL'ARETINA

Aretina-style roast rabbit

This dish was once the traditional Sunday lunch for families throughout the Tuscan countryside. Rabbit is still very popular today.

Preparation time: 20 minutes
Cooking time: 45 minutes
Serves 8

- 1 × 2.75-kg (6-lb) cleaned and skinned rabbit, liver and kidneys reserved
- 5 tablespoons olive oil
- 4–5 bacon rashers (slices), diced
- 1 clove garlic, chopped
- 1 sprig rosemary, chopped
- 175 ml (¾ cup) red wine
- 175 ml (¾ cup) chicken stock
- salt and pepper

Cut the rabbit into large pieces, halving the saddle and hind legs. Trim and slice the liver and kidneys. Heat the oil in a shallow pan. Mix together the bacon, garlic and rosemary, add to the pan and cook over low heat, stirring occasionally, for 5 minutes. Increase the heat to medium and add the pieces of rabbit, starting with the thighs, which take longer to cook. Cook, turning frequently, for 15 minutes, until evenly browned.

Season with salt and pepper. Stir in the liver and kidneys, drizzle with the wine and cook for a few minutes until the alcohol has evaporated. Reduce the heat and simmer, stirring occasionally, for 10–15 minutes, then remove the liver and kidneys from the pan and set aside. Pour in half the stock and cook the rabbit pieces for another 10–15 minutes, gradually adding the remaining stock.

Remove the pan from the heat and transfer the rabbit to a warmed serving dish. Transfer the cooking juices to a food processor or blender, add the liver and the kidneys and process to a purée. Scrape into a sauce boat and serve immediately with the rabbit.

FEGATELLI

Preparation time: 30 minutes + 1–2 hours for soaking
Cooking time: 8 minutes
Serves 4

Livers

- 300 g (11 oz) caul fat
- 600 g (1 lb 5 oz) pig's liver, trimmed
- 50 g (2 oz) (about 2 slices) lightly toasted white bread, grated
- ½ tablespoon fennel seeds
- 18 wild fennel or rosemary stems
- olive oil, for brushing
- salt and pepper

Cut the caul fat into 18 × 8-cm (3-inch) square pieces, put them into a bowl of warm water and let soak for 1–2 hours, until softened.

Cut the liver into 18 cubes, 3 cm (1¼ inches) on each side and season with salt and pepper. Mix together the breadcrumbs and fennel seeds in a shallow dish and season with salt and pepper. Roll the pieces of liver in the mixture to coat. Drain the squares of caul fat and squeeze out the excess moisture.

Wrap each coated cube of liver in a square of caul fat and secure them with the wild fennel stems.

Heat a griddle (grill) pan or heavy frying pan or skillet and brush with oil. Add the fegatelli and cook over medium heat, turning occasionally, for 6–8 minutes, until lightly browned. Serve immediately. You could also thread them onto skewers, alternating with cubes of bread and cubes of bacon, then cook them under the grill (broiler), turning occasionally and brushing them twice with oil, for 8 minutes.

Alternatively, the liver can also be prepared by chopping it finely, mixing it with a little grated toasted white bread and seasoning with salt and pepper. The mixture is shaped into small balls, wrapped in caul fat and threaded onto skewers, alternating with bay leaves, before grilling (broiling).

ZOLFINO BEANS

It is hard to imagine an image that better encapsulates the essence of Tuscan cuisine than a *fiasco* (glass flask), simmering gently overnight in the ashes of a dying fire. Its contents are a precious handful of zolfino beans, olive oil and herbs.

The zolfino bean *(fagiolo zolfino),* also known as sulphur beans, grows best in the hilly slopes next to the Strada Setteponti which winds along the ancient route of the Cassia Vetus. Growing the zolfino bean is a labour of love. Everything has to be done by hand, which means many hours of toil for a very low-yielding plant. Known also as the *fagiolo del cento* (bean of the hundred), the seeds are traditionally sown on the hundredth day of the year. But the outcome is far from certain because the zolfino bean is a particularly delicate plant — too much rain, or too much sun, and it dies. But the end result, as the zolfini farmers well know, is worth the effort. The reward is a bean with a very fine skin, making it easier to digest, yet which still holds its shape during cooking and has a flavour that is creamy yet also intensely tasty.

This page:
To capture the full flavour of zolfino beans, they are seasoned with olive oil and fresh herbs and cooked in a flask slowly over the dying coals of a fire.

Opposite page:
A *credenza* (kitchen cupboard) in a Tuscan kitchen should never be without staples such as dried pulses, home made olive oil and a bottle of Chianti wine.

FAGIOLI NEL 'FIASCO'

Beans in a flask

Traditionally, beans were cooked in a flask placed in a wood-fired bread oven. The flask was put into the oven as soon as the fire had gone out but while it was still very hot, and left overnight. The following morning the beans would be perfectly cooked.

Preparation time: 15 minutes + overnight soaking
Cooking time: 5 hours + 15 minutes standing time
Serves 6

- 500 g (2¾ cups) dried cannellini or zolfino beans, soaked overnight in water to cover and drained
- 100 ml (scant ½ cup) olive oil, plus extra for drizzling
- 1–2 cloves garlic
- 6 sage leaves
- 4 black peppercorns
- salt and pepper

Put the beans into a large heatproof bottle or flask, preferably with a wide opening, and add the oil, garlic, sage, peppercorns, a pinch of salt and sufficient water to cover them by 1 cm (½ inch). Fold a dish towel into several layers and put it into the bottom of a large pan.

Put the flask on top and pour in water to surround it. Cook over low heat for about 5 hours, adding more hot water to the pan as necessary. Do not add water to the flask of beans. When the beans are cooked, turn off the heat, let them stand for 15 minutes and then transfer to a warmed serving dish. Drizzle with olive oil, season to taste with salt and pepper and serve immediately.

INDEX

Page numbers in bold refer to the illustrations

Phaidon Press Limited
2 Cooperage Yard
London E15 2QR

Phaidon Press Inc.
111 Broadway
New York, NY 10006

Phaidon SARL
55, rue Traversière
75012 Paris

www.phaidon.com

First published 2011
Published in this format 2026

ISBN: 978 1 83729 245 5

Tuscany originates from *Il cucchiaio d'argento Cucina Regionale*, first published in 2008, and from *Il cucchiaio d'argento,* first published in 1950, eighth edition (revised, expanded and redesigned in 1997)

A CIP catalogue record for this book is available from the British Library.

Narrative text by Mario Matassa
Photographs by Edward Park
Illustrations by Beppe Giacobbe
Designed by Sonya Dyakova

Printed in China

The publishers would like to thank Alberto Bellotti, Hilary Bird, Sara Bryant, Mary Consonni, Clelia d'Onofrio, Linda Doeser, Carmen Figini, Jamie Hazeel, Silvia Marilli and Daniela Silva, for their contributions to the book.

RECIPE NOTES

Butter should always be unsalted.

Pepper is always freshly ground black pepper, unless otherwise specified.

Eggs, vegetables and fruits are assumed to be medium size, unless otherwise specified. For US, use large eggs unless otherwise specified.

Milk is always whole, unless otherwise specified.

Garlic cloves are assumed to be large; use two if yours are small.

Ham means cooked ham, unless otherwise specified.

Prosciutto refers exclusively to raw, dry-cured ham, usually from Parma or San Daniele in northern Italy.

Cooking and preparation times are for guidance only, as individual ovens vary. If using a fan oven, follow the manufacturer's instructions concerning oven temperatures.

To test whether your deep-frying oil is hot enough, add a cube of stale bread. If it browns in thirty seconds, the temperature is 180–190°C (350–375°F), about right for most frying. Exercise caution when deep frying: add the food carefully to avoid splashing, wear long sleeves, and never leave the pan unattended.

Some recipes include raw or very lightly cooked eggs. These should be avoided particularly by the elderly, infants, pregnant women, convalescents, and anyone with an impaired immune system.

All herbs, shoots, flowers and leaves should be picked fresh from a clean source.

Do exercise caution when foraging for ingredients, which should only be eaten if an expert has deemed them safe to eat. In particular, do not gather wild mushrooms yourself before seeking the advice of an expert who has confirmed their suitability for human consumption.

As some species of mushrooms have been known to cause allergic reaction and illness, do take extra care when cooking and eating mushrooms and do seek immediate medical help if you experience a reaction after preparing or eating them.

All spoon measurements are level.
1 teaspoon = 5 ml; 1 tablespoon = 15 ml.
Australian standard tablespoons are 20 ml, so Australian readers are advised to use 3 teaspoons in place of 1 tablespoon when measuring small quantities.

Cup, metric and imperial measurements are given throughout, and US equivalents are given in brackets. Follow one set of measurements, not a mixture, as they are not interchangeable.
